GIVE THEM SHELTER

Responding to Hunger and Homelessness

Michael J. Moran

Resurrection Press
Mineola, New York

Cover Design: Thomas Grasso

Cover Photo: "Rubin 1987" by Adrienne Thayer

Inside Photos:
    Michael Moran by Bill Heacock
    Pages 26, 46, 68, 82 and 90 by Adrienne Thayer
    Last photo by Kathy Howard Jacobsen

First published in 1990 by Resurrection Press, Ltd.
                            P.O. Box 248
                            Williston Park, NY 11596

Second Printing 1991

ISBN 0-9623410-6-1
Library of Congress Card Catalog Number 90-60442

Printed in the United States of America by Faith Printing.

This book is dedicated to

THE HUNGRY AND HOMELESS PEOPLE ON LONG ISLAND

. . . they are us, and we are them.

Acknowledgements

Wallie Lorthioir, Helen Meyer, Joan Jadge, faithful typists and technical consultants.

Emilie Teutschman, a kind and dedicated editor.

Pat Kollmer, Pat O'Connor, Jean Kelly, Maryellen Kane, and the Community with whom I live, for the inspiration of their ideas and their lives.

Michael Moran
Executive Director and Co-founder
Interfaith Nutrition Network

Table of Contents

Foreword

In the darkest days of the Nazi occupation of France, quiet heroes emerged as the forces of the Resistance. Heroism then, as now, arose from the small things. A half century after the Allies liberated Paris, Michael Moran's story of resistance to inhumanity on Long Island reminds us that at least some quiet heroes are still alive, still well and still desperately needed.

The tale of the INN is a simple one indeed. A group of suburban people, *very* suburban people, come together in concrete action against homelessness. There is nothing remarkable about this conspiracy; it is a tale of simple decencies in a world where people still matter.

The simplicity of this story belies its import. The last decade in America is a period of times gone mad. For the first time in our national history, mass homelessness came to co-exist with national prosperity. In times past it took the dislocations of war, famine, natural disaster or at least world-wide economic disorders to render millions of citizens homeless. The catastrophes of the 1980s were more subtle.

We depopulated psychiatric hospitals, but never sent the food and housing out to the community with the former patients. We repudiated with a radical fervor 50 years of bi-partisan federal housing policy, but we never considered where the poor children of our land would find shelter. We taught our own children how to shield their eyes from beggars on city streets and on nightly news reports, but we never figured out how to explain to our sons and daughters why we feed the family dog and walk past the old woman huddled on a steam grate.

The 1980s were not the best of times. Yet in the darkness and gloom the beacon of the INN shined bright.

Long Island is perhaps one of the oddest places left on earth, or so it seems to those of us reared in its comforting confines. Nassau and Suffolk Counties, the land where Michael Moran's battle rage, remain among the most affluent counties in America. To most, the Long Island of my childhood remains. Tree lined cul-de-sacs for touch football, Little League baseball and hard working, if at times struggling, families. Long Island may not be Richard Nixon's Peoria, but it is bedrock middle America. Or so we thought.

In fact, Long Island is streaked with pockets of poverty. Homeless people scrounge for survival in wooded lots and deserted train stations. And it can be a mean place. There is racism, there is escapism, and there is homelessness.

In the mid-1980s I found myself in federal court representing a homeless family from Nassau County living in a car in a shopping mall parking lot. I was stunned, as a lad who spent my first 22 years in a sleepy Long Island town, to be castigated as an outside agitator for daring to tell a judge that my home county, Nassau County, was not obeying the law and aiding homeless families.

Michael Moran, in the 1980s found himself at Hofstra University. He was supposed to be a chaplain. He was supposed to mind his own business. Instead, he committed the most frightening act allowed a man. He opened his eyes, he saw the imprint of human suffering and he did not look away. The harsh and terrible love of Dorothy Day seeped through Moran's fabric and permeated his being. Once he looked, once he saw, once he refused to turn away, he no longer was a free man. He was bound, without escape, to do battle against poverty. He took on the task of applying balm to the miserable, and his tale, the tale of the INN, is of course a story of love, joy and happiness.

The story of the INN is a moral tale to be sure. More than that, it's a reminder that one man can make a difference and goodness, like evil, will spread outward in ever-widening concentric circles.

If it took an era of gratuitous callousness in the 1980s to create mass homelessness, it also took an era of deprivation to ignite the noble forces that run as a stream somewhere through each community. Michael Moran turned that stream into a healing river.

In the 1930s Bertolt Brecht wrote of the Michael Morans who labored nightly to find beds for homeless men. "It won't change the world," wrote Brecht, "it won't end the age of exploitation, but for tonight, a man has a bed."

Bertolt Brecht was wrong, Michael Moran is changing the world. Thanks to him, we are a day closer to ending the age of exploitation. And Michael Moran's story, the tale of the INN, will change the world of those who read it and choose not to look away.

Robert M. Hayes, Founder
National Coalition for the Homeless
January 1990

Chapter 1

In The Beginning
There Was A Need

There is room at the INN. But that wasn't always the case here on Long Island, I remember when I first became involved with the issue of homelessness.

It was 1981 and I had recently been appointed as a chaplain at Hofstra University. I had just completed a job working with former mental patients, most of whom were economically disadvantaged but I never expected to find poor people living on Long Island. As I began my work at Hofstra, I was troubled. A good number of students had lots of pocket money, shiny Corvettes and vacationed in Acapulco. "If there's one thing I can do for these students," I said to myself, "it's to teach them how the other half lives." Indeed, many of the students had never seen, much less talked with a poor person.

I challenged a group of students to volunteer with me at a soup kitchen/shelter in Brooklyn. The place was called CHIPS (Christian Help in Park Slope). CHIPS was a storefront operation which served lunch to about 75 people a day and provided emergency shelter to 15 people overnight, including singles and families.

The students and I were so enriched by our first few experiences at this shelter that we decided to volunteer there one weekend a month.

Several months later I was sitting in my office at Hofstra when the phone rang. "Hi," she said, "my name is Pat O'Connor. I live down here in Cedarhurst. I heard what you're doing with those students at CHIPS, and I want to help."

"Oh," I said, "that's wonderful, Why don't you tell me something about yourself?"

Pat quickly replied, "I'm the mother of nine children but I have a little extra time on my hands and I want to help."

"This poor woman," I said to myself. "Imagine nine kids! Most women are having children; she's having a baseball team!" "Listen, Mrs. O'Connor," I said to her, "why don't you make a casserole and bring it over here? I'll take it to CHIPS the next time we go."

"Casserole!" she screamed. "I hate to cook and I'm a lousy cook at that. I want to go into Brooklyn and get my hands dirty. Just give me the address." I gave her directions and wished her well, figuring she'd go in once, get upset with what she found, and never go back.

Much to my surprise, Mother O'Connor went every Thursday for the next year. Can you imagine what job they gave her? She was in charge of the laundry—washing and drying the linens used on the cots the previous week. This indeed was cruel and unusual punishment for the mother of nine. But she did it faithfully every Thursday for the next year.

At the end of the year I was sitting at my desk at Hofstra. The phone rang and it was none other than Pat O'Connor.

"Michael," she said, in her direct and unaffected way, "we haven't met yet. I'm the crazy woman from Cedarhurst who hates cooking. I volunteer at CHIPS on Thursday and you go with the students on weekends." And then she exploded. "What the hell are we going into Brooklyn for when there's a need for a soup kitchen right here on Long Island?"

Now I was convinced there was something wrong with this woman. "Long Island," I replied, "Long Island is one of the most affluent areas in the country. There's no need for a soup kitchen here. Everyone's got a split-level home, two cars in the garage and 2.5 kids with their own fully-equipped room. Where do you see a need here?"

"Michael, did you ever go into Hempstead?"

"Not really," I said, "Hofstra is actually located in Hempstead but prides itself as being more in Uniondale."

"Michael, do me a favor. Go visit Hempstead."

That very afternoon I got in my car and drove into the heart of Hempstead. I parked my car in the A&S parking lot, walked along Fulton Avenue, toward the bus terminal, made my way to the Long Island Railroad station, hurried through Denton Green (the little park in the middle of the village) and made a B-line to my car and drove back to Hofstra.

I immediately telephoned Pat O'Connor. "You're right," I exclaimed. What I saw today can only be described as a social sin, a sin of our society, neglect for those in need. I witnessed too many hungry and homeless people. I was shocked to see so many women and children among their numbers. We have to do something about this human tragedy."

"You're on."

We made friends with Nancy Dwyer, a feature writer at the *Long Island Catholic*, a weekly newspaper. Nancy wrote a small article about two insane Long Islanders who wanted to open a soup kitchen in Hempstead. At the end of the piece she gave a phone number for anyone interested in helping us. Since I would be away when the article appeared, I gave my sister's phone number. My sister is a busy mother of seven, but I told her she'd only have two or three calls. After all, what well-to-do Long Islander would be interested in such a wild idea on rich Long Island?

When I returned from my Christmas trip, there was an urgent message: "Call your sister. She is going to kill you."

"Dorothy," I asked excitedly, "what happened?"

"My dear brother," she began calmly, "my phone has not stopped ringing. The world wants to open a soup kitchen and I'll be the first on line since I haven't had a chance to eat or drink with all these phone calls. But, you'll get yours now. Since I knew nothing about the project, I told them to call you beginning today." And at that, she hung up!

And call they did. All that afternoon and evening I was answering questions about a project I had only sketched out in my imagination. I made up the details as I went along, not wanting to lose the goodwill and assistance of all those potential volunteers.

Pat O'Connor and I set the first meeting for February 1, 1983 at the Hofstra campus parish house in Uniondale, THE HOUSE WHICH WOULD LATER BECOME OUR FIRST SHELTER FOR THE HOMELESS.

Thirty-five people showed up on that historic evening. These were people from all walks of life: clergy, business people, social workers, housewives and househusbands. As we went around the room for introductions, each person spoke of the need for a soup kitchen in Hempstead. We started to get excited about the project. One man stood up and said, "I know the idea is a good one and there's lots of energy here tonight, but I helped start a soup kitchen in Wyandanch and it took us a full year to get it off the ground. So let's cool our heels and take it slow." A senior citizen in the back of the room raised her hand and shouted, "A year! That's ridiculous. People are hungry right now. We have to feed them. Six months—we've got to open in six months."

There was such dynamic energy in this self-appointed group, and they worked so well together that the Hempstead soup kitchen opened exactly three months later on May 2, 1983. What a marvelous tribute to the dedication and hard work of those early pioneers.

Before documenting the steps taken to allow for such a rapid opening, I must tell you about one energetic woman present at the first meeting. Her name is Sandy Chapin, the widow of folk singer Harry Chapin.

Sandy is a prolific dreamer and innovator. This project really caught her imagination. As if looking through a crystal ball, she shouted, "We'll call this soup kitchen the Interfaith Nutrition Network, The INN. Churches and synagogues of all denominations will want to get involved. We'll serve nutritious meals. And we'll network all over Long Island." Sandy turned out to be a real prophet. In truth, many religious congregations have been involved; the meals are hearty and plentiful and we have networked all over Nassau and Suffolk, with 16 soup kitchen locations presently in operation.

Sandy continued her creative rampage. "The INN!" she exclaimed. "Unlike the Bethlehem Inn, there will be room for everybody. And unlike Gurney's Inn at Montauk Point, you won't have to pay a fortune to eat there. As a matter of fact the homeless won't have to pay a cent, nor will anyone get paid." True to her dream, today we serve over 1,200 free meals each day and we can boast of more than 1,100 volunteers—none of whom get paid for their many hours of service.

Armed with a name for our soup kitchen, the planning group was now ready to do all the necessary groundwork in preparation for the opening of the Hempstead INN.

First, a committee was established to substantiate the need for a soup kitchen in Hempstead. Were there really enough hungry and homeless people to justify the opening of such a facility? Would the churches and synagogues cooperate when they knew of the urgency and the numbers in need?

What better way to find out than to ask them? And so, a committee of the originators set about visiting every house of worship in the Village of Hempstead, thirty-five in all. They asked the pastor, priest or rabbi: "Do you think there's a need here in the village for a soup kitchen?"

"No doubt about it," was the response. "The hungry and homeless in increasing numbers are coming to my door. They need food, clothing, shelter. There's definitely a need."

"Well, Pastor (Rabbi, Father)," continued the committee spokesperson, "if you really believe there's a need, could you help us get started? Put a few lines in your bulletin describing our intention to open a soup kitchen and ask for volunteers to call us."

"Sure," they said, "that's the least we can do."

"Another way you can help us, if you really believe in the idea, is to give us a money donation to help us get started, you know, to buy some food and equipment, pay the rent, etc."

"OK, we can help you with some seed money."

Looking curiously at their surroundings, the INN representative asked, "You wouldn't happen to have an extra kitchen and dining room we could use as the soup kitchen would you?"

"No, no, no," shouted the clergy, "My facility is used to the maximum. We operate on a full schedule; all rooms are used constantly."

NIMBY

The committee learned their lesson: support, money and prayers are in great measure but once it gets too close to home, the NIMBY (not in my back yard) syndrome takes over. The founders of The INN soon learned the bitter reality: although nearly everybody wants a soup kitchen, no one wants one in their neighborhoods.

It was the thirty-fourth house of worship they visited, Unity Church of Hempstead, located in the center of the village at Fulton Avenue and Main Street, which turned out to be the key to the fulfillment of the dream. The black woman pastor, Ida Bowles, said, "Why not! The congregation and I have been thinking of doing something like that for a while now. We have a newly equipped kitchen and freshly decorated dining room. Let's get started." Blessings upon you, Ida, you took a risk too many of your colleagues refused! We salute you and your congregation. The dream could indeed become a reality.

Progress was being made on all sides. Volunteers and money started pouring in from churches, synagogues and individuals, both from the local area and from all over Nassau County.

Opening Day

We were ready to open. Jean Kelley organized and trained volunteers so well, food and money donations were so plentiful, and the willing spirit of so many was in such large measure that after just three months in preparation, the Hempstead INN proudly opened its doors on May 2, 1983.

I'll never forget that first day. Everything was in place. About 15 volunteers showed up to prepare and serve a delicious spaghetti meal. Sister Irene Scarola and I took our places at the front door to act as greeters. On the dot of twelve we opened the door to ten people. We had more volunteers than guests! "Well," we said to each other, "the invited guests have not arrived. Let's go out to the highways and byways and invite others to the feast!" And so we did. We walked across the street to the park, the bus terminal, the Long Island Railroad station and invited anyone who looked like they needed our hospitality. You should have seen the surprised look on their faces. In our society, money talks and very little comes free. Yet here we were inviting people for a free meal. "Are you for real?" asked one man. "You must be from some church looking for fresh converts." We managed to round up another twenty guests or so and the feast was under way!

Word of mouth spread on the street (that's our best public relations system): "Good food and you don't have to pray with them or read the Bible." Within one week we were feeding fifty; within one month, one hundred. Now, seven years later, we feed a nutritious, hearty lunch to more than two hundred people each day at the Hempstead INN.

What It Takes

What are the main ingredients in running a soup kitchen? I think they are volunteers, food, donations, prayers and, of course, hungry people—our guests. Given those we still need a place. Whenever I give a talk on Long Island about the problem of homelessness, I ask the audience to imagine that we are opening a soup kitchen in their town. I'm quick to say, "Don't worry we're not about to do that." Here, the strained faces relax into smiles. God forbid it should happen in their neighborhood! As they call out the list of items needed for a soup kitchen, invariably the audience omits "hungry people." I point out this oversight and just as quickly suggest the reason: I think most people forget there are hungry people right in their midst, or they don't want to admit it.

Let's look at our first necessity—volunteers. Without this precious commodity, The INN would not have survived. They are the mainstay of our effort.

They come to us from churches and synagogues on Long Island, from community service clubs, civic associations, and as individuals. The best recruiting method is word of mouth; a satisfied volunteer will bring in his or her relative, neighbor or friend.

Last year I gave over 100 talks about The INN, mostly to church and synagogue groups. The initial reaction to my speech is,

"You're exaggerating. There's no hunger on Long Island. Sure, we see it on TV as the cameras pan Penn Station. But not here—not on affluent Long Island. Many of us moved here to escape those problems. Don't tell us the problems are following us here."

"Yes," I tell them, "there are hungry and homeless people on Long Island, and the number is growing." In fact, the Nassau Suffolk Coalition for the Homeless estimates that there are approximately 30,000 homeless people on Long Island, 15,000 in Nassau and 15,000 in Suffolk. Now the New York State Department of Social Services' definition for "homeless" is "persons who do not reside in their own domicile." This includes people living on the street, in cars and vans, in abandoned buildings. This number includes about 10,000 people. The others are doubled-up, tripled-up, quadrupled-up, often in unsanitary, overcrowded, unsafe living conditions. Many are on the verge of eviction. When I tell my audiences these awful facts, and when they hear my first-hand stories about the homeless, they are quick to believe, to donate and even better—to volunteer. Thus, we presently number 1,100 volunteers in our soup kitchens and shelters.

Our volunteers are interviewed by a member of the staff and given on-site training. They are often put on the front lines their first day at work. "We need someone to do the pots," and there goes another new volunteer being given "on the job training." Basically, our volunteers come one day a week, from 10 a.m. to 1:30 p.m. They help prepare the meal, butter the bread, roll the plastic cutlery in paper napkins, prepare the coffee and dessert table, say a short interfaith prayer and open the doors at the dot of noon. They serve our guests from 12 noon to 1:00 p.m. and then clean up.

The most important qualities of our volunteers are their ability to treat our guests as equals, to be flexible and to have a good sense of humor! I'll never forget Edith. She came to us from St. Joseph's Church in Garden City. On her first day she was shocked to find that The INN was not a Catholic agency. All her married life she had done volunteer work in her own parish, rubbing shoulders with other Catholics. Now she was working hand to hand with Jews, Buddhists, Protestants, Bahai's and people of no religion at all. At first I noticed that Edith and the other volunteers hardly spoke to each other as they prepared the meal in the kitchen. One day I realized why this was so: like Edith, each had volunteered only in his/her church. Since we are taught never to argue about religion or politics, they were keeping to themselves! As time went on, however, they began conversing, even sharing religious stories, beliefs and practices. Soon they learned how much they had in common spiritually, and they realized that they shared a special common creed: they were there to feed hungry people. This is a religious act of the highest caliber. The Jews know it, as it is reflected so often in their scripture. Yahweh is always seen as the one who cares for the outcasts, the fringe people. At the annual Seder feast, Jews are encouraged to set an extra place at their family table for the stranger, the widow, the poor neighbor. And Christians cannot turn a page of their scripture without witnessing Jesus and his special outreach to the disenfranchised of his society. He is always curing, ministering to those people rejected by the civic and religious leaders of his time. He so identified with the outcasts that Matthew 25 carries this story of the final judgement. "Jesus will say to the just: 'Come into the Reign of God for I was hungry and you fed me, naked and you clothed me, homeless and you sheltered me.' And the people will say, 'Jesus, when did we see you in those terrible states?' And Jesus will say, 'As often as you did it to one of these, the most vulnerable of my sisters and brothers, you did it to me.' "

How can Jews or Christians live up to the most sacred lessons of their religion and turn their backs on God's favorites? Truly the rejected are such for our God has a preferential option for poor people.

I used to think that religion would be the salvation of the poor. I now believe the poor will be the salvation of religion. There are too many hungry and homeless people with us today. If our churches and synagogues turn them away, we are nothing but hypocrites. We must join forces and help eradicate hunger and homelessness in this wealthy nation. And that's what our volunteers try to do.

As for Edith, she broke through the religion barrier and began conversing with the other volunteers, and one day she said enthusiastically, "This is the best ecumenical movement I've ever seen. We are ministering together to hurting people. What better way to live out our various creeds!"

Once Edith reached this insight, she was delighted. But there was still one obstacle to overcome. Edith was afraid of the guests. You see, when Edith was a small girl her mother had told her, "Daughter, stay away from people who are different from you. They'll hurt you." And so Edith feared our guests, who were black, Hispanic and poor white.

It was about six months after Edith began volunteering that I spied her coming out of the kitchen with a cup of coffee in her hand. She carefully placed the coffee on a table and sat down across from a black welfare mother and her two children. They talked for about twenty minutes, and then she came over to me. "Michael," she began, "I'm shocked. When I was a little girl Mom told me to avoid people like this. She said they were too different and we'd have nothing in common. And for years I obeyed her. But today I asked myself, 'What's to fear?' Just now I sat down with a woman who from all natural appearances is totally different than I. But as we talked and shared our life stories, I'm stunned at how alike we are. We believe the same things about God, our country, the way we want to see our kids grow up. We're actually more alike than different. I'm shocked—but I'm no longer afraid." From then on, Edith chatted freely with our guests in this classroom of life where she learned, and grew, and shared, and became the Christian she always wanted to be.

This is the same lesson learned by multitudes of our volunteers: "I came to help others, but they are helping me more than I could ever assist them. They are opening my mind and heart to the realities of poverty in our country. I used to have stereotypes about the homeless. You know—they are all Bowery bums, alcoholics, able-bodied men who are too lazy to work. My volunteer work at The INN has proven those ideas to be myths. When I take the time to sit and talk with our guests, I look into their eyes and hearts. I see the victims of our system, the system I've loved and supported all my life. My cold heart is touched and this heart of stone becomes a heart of flesh. They do more for me than I could ever do for them."

Yes, these stories of conversion echo so often in our soup kitchens. What are the truths our volunteers are learning from their hands-on work with the homeless? Here are some of them:

1. Of the 30,000 homeless people on Long Island, two-thirds are women and children; half are under the age of 30.
2. One of the main causes of homelessness is the lack of permanent, low-cost housing for poor people.
3. The minimum wage is so low that if a person worked 40 hours a week for a whole year, their take-home pay would be less than $7,000. When it is increased in 1991, take-home will be about $9,000. How can one afford to live on Long Island either as a single or, much worse, with a family?
4. There is inadequate day care for our single parents, so a woman can't work because she must stay home and take care of the children.
5. Racism is a serious sin on Long Island. Available rental space for blacks is strictly limited to certain areas and neighborhoods. And let's face it, most landlords do not want a woman on welfare with three children.

These brutal lessons are learned by our volunteers as they take the time to listen to the painful stories of our guests.

Brenda

Brenda is the mother of three small preschoolers. Because the availability of day care is inadequate on Long Island, and also over-priced for poor people, Brenda cannot work but must be with her children all day, every day. One day I said to Brenda, "I see you at the soup kitchen almost every day. How are you doing?"

"Not well," she answered. "You know I'm on welfare. My husband left me and the three kids a number of years ago. Being on welfare, I get a check each moth to pay my rent."

"I'm sure that's a help."

"Not really," replied Brenda. "They give me $331 a month for a family of four to pay the rent. Have you ever tried to find a decent apartment for $331? Let me tell you the facts. First off, I'm black, so the area I can live in is very limited. Landlords don't want kids, especially when the mom is on welfare. Despite all this, I found a place. It's a single room, and we share a refrigerator and bathroom in the hall with three other families. The roaches are ready to unite and carry off the place. And for this gem we're paying $450 a month."

"How do you do it," I said, "if welfare only gives you $331? How do you make up the difference?"

"Well," she mused, "I have to take money from my food budget to pay the rent. That's why you see us here so often."

This is a common story I hear. The rents are so high that more and more people are using food money to pay the rent so they don't get evicted. That's why our soup lines are growing so rapidly.

"Well," I said, "can you make ends meet then?"

"Weekdays we can, but weekends when I know we won't have enough to eat, I prepare dinner, we all sit down at the table, and I feed the baby first, then the two-year-old, then the four-year-old, and if there is enough left over, I eat."

This is a shocking, immoral story. One I've heard too often at the soup kitchens.

Ben

Ben is 72 years old and with the help of his cane, walks a mile each day to eat at the soup kitchen. One day I asked, "How are you doing, Ben?"

"OK" he said, but I suspected he was hiding something.

"What's up?" I asked.

"Well," Ben answered sheepishly, "to tell you the truth, Michael, I have some food at home I could eat. But, you know I'm 72 and I live alone. When I prepare a meal and sit down by myself to eat it, ah—I don't feel like eating. But I come here and we sit and talk, and laugh and cry together, then I feel like eating."

John

John is 18 years old. His parents threw him out of the house when he was 16. He caused problems at home and in school. Borderline academically, John was always looking for attention in inappropriate ways.

"Where did you go when you were forced from your house?" I asked John.

"I stayed with different friends until their parents got tired of me and I had to move on."

"Where did you go then?"

"I'd stay in laundry rooms of apartment houses, or in abandoned cars or houses in Hempstead. Sometimes I'd climb into Salvation Army clothing drops and pile the clothes on top of me so I wouldn't freeze. Other times I'd go to the Nassau County Medical Center emergency room and along with many other homeless people, we'd pretend to be patients waiting to be seen. But when they discovered we weren't really ill, they'd call the police and have us evicted."

Quite frankly, I didn't know whether or not to believe John until one day I took the garbage to the backyard of our soup kitchen located on Fulton Avenue in Hempstead. There, to my amazement, were cardboard boxes set up, the kind large kitchen appliances are packed in. I looked inside this series of boxes and found a homeless family hovering together there in the cold. And this in the middle of February, in the middle of Nassau County where, according to some of our elected officials, we do not have a problem of hunger and homelessness!

Dorothy

Dorothy is a woman in her sixties. Very often when she came to eat at the soup kitchen, she'd ask for a bag of groceries to take home. Sometimes the volunteers would notice that she'd ask other people at lunch to take a bag and give it to her. We didn't know what she could possibly be doing with all these canned goods. Was she opening her own supermarket and making money on The INN? We became very suspicious and sometimes even refused her persistent requests for a care package to take home.

One day the mystery was solved. A young handicapped man said to a volunteer, "Isn't she a great woman? We call her Mom. She takes all that food and when she collects enough, she cooks a big meal and invites everyone in who doesn't have enough to eat. That's a pretty big family in her little apartment."

We bowed our heads at hearing this, so guilty of our unfounded suspicions and so admiring of "Mom Dorothy." Needless to say, she never again had to ask for a care package!

Good Samaritans

People often ask, "Where do you get your food?" Well, I must say, the amount of food wasted in this country is a social sin. In catering halls and restaurants when a party is over, those big trays of lasagna and other delicacies are thrown in the dumpster. It's the easiest way to get rid of the food. Meanwhile, people all over the country are going hungry.

We decided we would tap into as much of that wasted food as possible. So, volunteers visited their local bakeries, restaurants, farmstands, caterers, super-markets, etc. In many cases they were turned away because the owner feared lawsuits. Many don't know about the Good Samaritan law which states that donors of food to groups such as The INN will not be held liable for tainted foods. Rather, The INN is held responsible. Thank God, we have never had to face a lawsuit for food poisoning. Jokingly I tell our volunteers, "Now before serving the food, designate one worker to taste all of it. This way, if we are sued for food poisoning, we can always say, "Well, look at our volunteer who tested the same food, she's still alive!"

Many sources have taken the risk and donate food on a regular basis. Bakers, for instance, hate to see their works of art thrown away. Therefore, once they agree to help us, they take any leftovers (products not sold) and at the end of the day freeze the bread and cake and once a week a volunteer picks up the baked goods. We now have so many baked goods from so many generous bakers that I often say to our volunteers, "Let them eat cake!"

Farmstands have been good suppliers to The INN. One local place, in particular, used to throw away twenty-five cases of fruit and vegetables a week. A little brown on the lettuce, some spots on the apples, and out they'd go. We persuaded the owner to save the produce and each week a volunteer picks up the leftovers. Our volunteers go through the cases for what is salvageable. And there is more edible produce there than meets the eye. Many a hearty soup was created out of donated produce.

We also visited caterers and restaurants. Some were willing to help. The Garden City Hotel, for example, is one of our providers. When I first approached the manager to help us, I asked him, "What do you do with the leftovers from the big wedding parties you host?" He looked surprised. "We never have leftovers." (A common response from chefs who want to keep their jobs.) I looked at him knowingly and he said, "OK, we throw away the leftover food."

"Don't do that," I said, "just down the road from here we are feeding two hundred hungry people every day." He was shocked and agreed to donate his leftovers on a trial basis. It's a bit ironic, though. We receive the leftovers each Monday from the $32-a-place Sunday Brunch. Our guests come in and typically exclaim, "Pate and melon soup again!" We say, "Shut up and eat the caviar!" And they eat that horrible food because they're hungry!

Other food began to come our way by word of mouth. Parish and synagogue events where food was served became a source. Do you know how many parish picnics there are? And, oh, how we pray for rain!

People who had parties in their own homes would call and ask if we wanted the leftovers. Food would come in from weddings, bar mitzvahs, confirmations. Once we got a complete wedding cake and wondered all week what happened to the bride and groom. A priest had his ordination party and we were blessed with the leftovers.

Several years ago a woman called me and asked, "Would you like the leftovers from my wedding?"

"Of course, we would," I said.

"The food is a bit different though. It's health food."

"No problem," I gulped, "our guests will eat healthy food for a change!" And the very next morning she appeared (rice still in her hair) to make an offering of leftovers from her own wedding party. How wonderful people are! Here was a woman who, even on her wedding day, was concerned about people who did not have enough to eat.

All these donations are a real challenge to our daily volunteer cooks. They come in, do a careful inventory of the refrigerators and freezers, as well as the canned food stock, and create a balanced, nutritious, attractive meal. God bless the ingenuity of our chefs!

With all this food being served at the soup kitchen, people have often asked me, "What's your screening process? How do you know they all need and deserve a free meal? How do you weed out the cheats?"

The Golden Rule at The INN is that everyone gets served—no questions asked. The people who are our guests get hassled enough at the Department of Social Services, clinics, cheese give-away programs and food banks. Why compound this type of treatment? The food is given to us as donations. God provides. It's our job to feed hungry people no matter what their state of need. If a person is willing to stand on a line of up to 200 people for a meal, there must be a legitimate problem, be it economic, physical or emotional. Finally, I tell those who question our lack of screening, "You know, when Jesus fed the 5,000 on the hillside he didn't first make them fill out a questionnaire. He fed them! That's our job and the great blessing God has given us—to offer them a meal."

Two Prodigal Sons

On these long soup kitchen lines, I have met so many hurting people. Among them two young men come to mind whom I call my "two prodigal sons." One made it and the other has yet to make it.

Larry ate each day in our Hempstead INN. He was a friendly young man of about 24 years of age. His good looks were disguised behind a face bloated from alcohol. He drank every day—cheap wine and whiskey. He was homeless and would sleep wherever he could, with friends or under the stars. His personal hygiene was bad. How I wanted to put him in a tub and let him sit all day!

One day I spotted him weaving along Franklin Street. I stopped the car and invited him in. He looked so disgusted with himself and with life in general. "Larry," I asked him, "what's the story? How have you ended up in this rut?"

He told me of his early life. His father is the owner of a construction firm and always kept the family well housed and well fed. When Larry finished school he started working for his Dad. However, he could never do any job right, at least not in his father's estimation. Larry took to drinking on weekends. Then, he started hitting the bottle week nights too. He began missing days at work because he was hung over. Finally his father fired him and threw him out of the house. "That was two years ago," said Larry. "I've been bouncing around ever since."

"Do you want to stop drinking?" I asked.

"More than anything else. I want to get into a program. I need to get away somewhere to a hospital. But I can't because my clothing and possessions are at my friend's house. If I go away I know when I return they'll all be gone. And they're the only things I own."

I decided to call his bluff and shoot a hole in his lame excuse. "I'll make a deal with you," I said. "If I store your belongings and arrange for you to get into a program, will you go?" He hesitated, then said, "Yes, but let's do it before I change my mind."

We had to act quickly. I drove him to his friend's house right away. We loaded all his clothes and boxes into my trunk and immediately went to Mercy Hospital detox.

When I saw Larry the next day he was having a hard time but knew this is what he must do. "Thanks, Mike, for bringing me here. I couldn't have done it on my own," he said sheepishly.

Two weeks later he was transferred to a six-month residential treatment center in Plainview. When I visited him there he looked stronger. Larry had lost the bloatedness and his cuts and bruises from drunken falls were healing nicely. Six months later, I attended his graduation. How proud I was of him!

It's been five years since that great day and every year at the same time I get a call from him. "Mike," he says, "I'm celebrating my anniversary of being sober. Will you come to the AA party?" I go, thanking God for giving Larry the strength to begin again. The Prodigal Son has returned and is doing fine. So fine, as a matter of fact, that recently we invited him to become a member of the Advisory Board of The INN.

And then there was Lazarus, another Prodigal Son. Great name, I thought. For sure with a name like that he could easily be resurrected!

I first met him sitting outside my office. "I'm so hungry," he said. "The soup kitchen is closed, but couldn't I please have something to eat?" There was an irresistible smile on the angelic face of this 21-year-old.

"The soup kitchen is only open from 12 to 1 o'clock and it's 2 o'clock now," I replied.

"Oh, please, just a sandwich."

I couldn't resist. "OK, let's go."

I brought him to the soup kitchen and found some iced tea and fried chicken in the refrigerator. I sat across from him as he attacked the food. "Why are you so hungry?" I asked.

"My Mom threw me out of the house last night."

"Why?"

"I don't know."

"Yes, of course," I replied, "mothers always evict their kids for no reason."

"All right, I'll tell you. I've been on crack for four months now (later I found out it was really eight months) and she's gotten tired of trying to wake me up for work each day. I go out every night and meet friends and we smoke and I don't get home until dawn. Then I can't wake up. I've lost so many jobs. I need to get into a program."

"Perfect entry point," I said to myself. "I know a great program. Will you go?" He looked at me, half unbelieving, but said, "Yes, it's the only way out of this."

I drove him to Family Service Association, where he was interviewed immediately. The counselor said there was a waiting list for the substance abuse residential program.

"Where will I stay in the meanwhile?" Lazarus asked. "I slept in the park last night for the first time in my life. I was scared to death. My mother won't take me back and I've exhausted the invitations of friends. I can't sleep out again."

I said to the counselor, "Look, I'll put him up at our shelter until a program opens up, if you think he would be worth the risk."

"They're all worth the risk," he replied.

I picked up Laz, threw his bike on the back of my car and off we went to the shelter. He did fine the first night, even smiling as I told him his house job was to sweep and mop the kitchen floor. He got to bed early and the next morning was off to the Department of Social Services to open up his case and establish himself on Medicaid so that he would be able to get into a residential treatment program.

When he returned to the shelter that night he was obviously pleased with himself. "I think I'll make it," he said. But then it all came down on him. Around 11 o'clock he got the urge, left the house on his bike and didn't return until 1 a.m., three hours past curfew. I woke him up at 8 a.m. and almost cried as I told him, "Laz, you messed up. Sorry, you have to go." He simply acknowledged my words, hung his head and left.

I felt like such a heel, such a failure. But that's tough love. Maybe Laz has to really hit bottom. Perhaps he has to sleep out in the park many more nights, feel the hunger and the cold, and then maybe he'll be ready to help himself.

Laz, wherever you are tonight, I still love you. I'm here, ready to help, when you really want to help yourself. Forgive my seeming coldness. Lazarus, come out of the tomb!

Trouble at The INN

Don't think for a moment that we haven't had our share of troubles.

The very first day we opened our Hempstead soup kitchen a representative from the Department of Health showed up at the front door. The co-founder of The INN, Pat O'Connor, answered the door. (Pat is always being chided because of her Gracie Allen responses. For example, one time on a radio interview the MC asked her, "Now Pat, tell us what the soup kitchen is like." Without thinking, in her usual stream of consciousness manner, she replied, "Well, you know, we have tables and we have chairs...!")

The health inspector had a copy of the morning paper which featured a story on the opening of the soup kitchen and a picture of Pat O'Connor. The inspector asked, "Is this your picture over the story of the opening of a soup kitchen, for which you have not applied to the Department of Health?" Pat looked at him, looked at the newspaper, and blurted out, "That's not such a bad picture of me, is it?" The inspector did his thing and left us with a list of irregularities which needed fixing.

From time to time we have a problem with an obstreperous guest, sometimes high or intoxicated, who causes a ruckus. Occasionally we have had to call the police to remove a problem person so order could be restored. Usually our volunteers can handle the problem before it reaches this stage. Generally, we find our women volunteers are much better than the men in calming down a disorderly guest. Men too often present a macho challenge to our male guests. The women know how to handle the men. The older the woman, the better. And it's inevitably the older women who have been through hard times, perhaps the Depression itself, who can truly empathize with our guests. They know what it's like to have been hungry and to do without. They have been there, so they can relate to our hurting guests on an equal plane.

One woman who fits this description is Audrey. She's 82 years old and volunteers every Friday at our Hempstead soup kitchen. She's a fiesty, gregarious woman who often sneaks out back for a smoke just before the guests arrive. Her job is greeter and troubleshooter when necessary. Now Audrey stands all of five feet tall and it's often comical to see her standing beside a 6'5" man, with her finger pointed up at him, warning him to behave himself or "there'll be trouble." The burly, outspoken lion invariably melts and becomes like a lamb. Audrey then takes him by the hand and leads him gently to his place at the table.

Our worst problem at Hempstead during our early years was eviction. Yes, The INN kept getting evicted. We got bounced from one church to another each year for our first three years, and then we got ousted from town! You see, everyone wants a soup kitchen, but not in their neighborhood. The churches which hosted our ministry did so initially in response to the Gospel mandate, "Feed the hungry." They thought it was a good idea to follow Jesus. But, when they saw the fringe people arrive and smelled them, that was too much. We receive as our guests many of the societal outcasts with whom Jesus associated. We have our share of alcoholics, drug addicts, prostitutes, transvestites—the folks Jesus would be walking and talking with if he were here now.

Unfortunately, our middle-class host churches were not prepared for this. Besides, they were getting grief from the local merchants and neighbors who were disturbed over the 100 to 200 people on the street outside their church. The mayor, too, was upset. After all, no mayor likes to admit that he has hungry people in his town. It doesn't look good for his administration. Nor does it provide the best image if one is trying to upgrade the town and bring in new business and folks who might "gentrify" the place.

So The INN didn't last more than a year in each of its first three locations before we were evicted. (Actually, it was a good experience for the soup kitchen to be "homeless;" it gave us a taste of what our guests must go through when they are evicted and must constantly relocate.)

After our third eviction—from a site called Church of the Happy Heart, which turned out to be the most unhappy heart I have ever experienced—we could not find another church or synagogue in the village of Hempstead to take us in.

Finally, we ended up taking our show on the road and at the eleventh hour, just as we were about to close up for good, I discovered a pastor in Freeport who was ready and willing to offer us a place in his church.

On the last day in Hempstead we tried to explain our reason for leaving town to the 150 people we fed that day. We promised to return as soon as we could. We really believed that and so did our guests.

Chapter 2

"Soup's On"
All Over Long Island

Other communities on Long Island learned about
The INN. Grassroots groups of people came to us and
said, "We heard about The INN and the work you are
doing. We want to do something similar in our town.
Could you help us get started?" I emphasize that these
were grassroots people. It was never the mayor or the city
council or the civic associations. Just ordinary people who
saw a need and wanted to respond to it.

How could The INN say no? We had sufficient funds,
we knew how to get food and monetary donations, we had
some experience in recruiting and training volunteers.
We were in a good position to reach out to other groups
desirous of opening soup kitchens.

Here is the process we used in assisting other groups.
First, we would meet with the small core group which
identified the problem. They would already be getting
flack from the local elected officials and merchants.
Sometimes, believe it or not, even the churches would be
objecting. People are often fearful that if you open a soup
kitchen, it will bring in an "undesirable element" (translated God's favorites) from outside the area. On the con-
trary, we found that when we open a soup kitchen, the
people served are always the local residents, some of
whom have been living on the edge for years. Some are
the "new poor," the senior citizens, those for whom the
rising cost of living is too much to bear, and the individuals losing their jobs and sometimes their homes due
to lack of funds. These are the local people a soup kitchen
feeds.

At our first meeting with this core group, we suggest

ways in which they could document the need for a soup kitchen in their area. (At first The INN tried to find a new word for "soup kitchen," a term which is a leftover from the days of the depression. We attempted to introduce the phrase "public dining room." However, it never caught on. People know exactly what you mean when you say soup kitchen. Everyone, that is, except my Vietnamese refugee friend who always insisted that when I was saying "soup kitchen" I was really trying to say "chicken soup." For him that was more acceptable!)

To establish the need for such a site, I'd recommend that a committee visit the churches and synagogues and ask if they were being regularly visited by people in need of food, clothing and shelter. The local social service agencies (Salvation Army, St. Vincent de Paul, Lutheran Community Services) are also good sources of information on the number of economically hurting people in the area. We would give the committee one month to do this investigation and report back to the group with the results. Certainly we would not want to be so self-indulgent in fulfilling our own needs as to establish a soup kitchen where there were no hungry people. Another result of making local contact is to engage the assistance of the local congregations and the social service agencies from the start. They are an invaluable reservoir of assistance: volunteers, money, food, public relations, etc.

If the church or synagogue was really seeing the need, based on the numbers of people who came to their doors, the canvasser asked the clergyperson, "If we do establish such a facility, would you and your congregation be able to assist us with volunteers and monetary contributions—seed money to get us off the ground?"

Once the need for a soup kitchen was firmly established, our core committee would write to all the churches and synagogues in the area asking them to place an announcement in their bulletin, such as the following:

Local group seeks to establish Soup Kitchen
to feed the hungry. Come to a meeting
at St. John's Church auditorium on
Tues., Oct. 4 - 8:00 P.M.
to find out how you can help.

For more information call
The INN—486-8506

The night of the kick-off meeting always turns out to be a blast. At two of our locations, Huntington and Glen Cove (yes, the awareness of homelessness has finally hit Long Island's Gold Coast, the North Shore), more than 150 local people showed up at each meeting. And they were not there to protest the opening of such a facility, but to offer their voluntary services! What a boost to the morale of those in the group: so many neighbors who realized there's a need in the community. What a compliment to the social awareness of grassroots people: individuals who see a need and really want to make a difference in their own community.

At the initial meeting of interested volunteers, I'd give a brief history of The INN and explain how our agency could assist the group. Next, a report from the committee which studied the local needs would be given. As they intuitively knew, the local churches, synagogues and social service agencies have seen a great number of homeless people and want to help in the establishment of a soup kitchen. A vote of the assembled people is then taken. "Do you believe there is a need in the community for a soup kitchen?" With an overwhelming majority voting "yes," we next ask them if they are prepared to help. Again we are blessed with affirmations.

It is now time to put them to work. I explain the need to establish working committees to begin preparations for the opening of a soup kitchen. The following committees are established that very first night.

Site Committee. This committee has the most difficult job of all—to get a church to commit its facility to a soup kitchen. Most of our soup kitchens are located in churches of all denominations. These sites are usually equipped with a large commercial kitchen and a big dining hall. Having a soup kitchen in a church usually brings community acceptance we would not find in another type of facility. After all, the church is simply fulfilling its scriptural mission to reach out and serve the most vulnerable in the community. Here is a hands-on way to apply the principles of the Hebrew and Christian scriptures to the life of the church and synagogue. Often,

- 29 -

an added attraction is the fact that the church or synagogue realizes it will not be acting alone, but rather in concert with other local congregations—a real interfaith effort.

Volunteers must go out into the community to find an appropriate place for the soup kitchen. Many a parish council has fought over this one. More often than not, the congregation questions the kind of people who will come to eat in their church. We fear that people who are different from us will hurt us in some way. "It's OK to help the hungry, but not here." Perhaps that is why it's easier to send money to the foreign missions, fulfilling my obligation, but I don't have to see poor people up close.

However, the committee has never failed. In each town or village there has always been one church willing to take the plunge, sometimes risking community opposition and suffering the complaints of local merchants and elected officials. But, as people of faith, they have taken the leap and opened their door to "God's favorites."

Food Committee. These volunteers are commissioned to go into the vineyard and collect the leftovers. They make contact with local bakers, caterers, restaurateurs, farmstands and supermarket owners and beg leftovers on a regular basis. They encourage local churches and synagogues to donate money and to provide prepared foods and desserts for the soup kitchen. This committee must also find the best food distributor for purchasing food in bulk. When a site has been chosen, this committee must also check the storage, refrigeration and freezer capacity to be sure these are adequate.

Volunteer Committee. This group of people must recruit volunteers (usually through local churches and synagogues) and provide for the training and supervision of all new volunteers.

Public Relations Committee. These folks must decide the most appropriate way to garner community, religious and political support for the soup kitchen. It's a matter of individually visiting the key players. They must also plan to make use of the media to inform the public and win support.

Finance Committee. These people seek monetary contributions from religious congregations, merchants and individuals. They are responsible for fund raising, establishing a bank account and the budgeting of money. With the assistance of The INN's main office, they locate and apply for special grants from banks, corporations and family foundations.

Steering Committee. Volunteers for this committee oversee the entire project and comprise the executive board. They conduct elections for the officers (President, Vice President, Secretary and Treasurer) and plan the agenda for general meetings. The chairperson of each of the working committees mentioned above is a member of the steering committee.

These committees are put to work immediately. They are commissioned to meet at least once, or as many times as necessary between general meetings, which are held once every three or four weeks.

Usually the group is enthusiastic and wants to open the kitchen immediately. I impress upon them that very much depends on how energetically the committees apply themselves to the tasks at hand. This will determine how rapidly the soup kitchen will open.

There is room for volunteers to join any committee, and all are encouraged to do so. It's the active participation during planning which establishes the enthusiastic base for the project.

All are encouraged to pray for the success of this important work. All meetings open with an interfaith prayer. This is the prime basis for our work and it is the interfaith spirit which eventually leads to a successful opening of the soup kitchen.

Here is a sample prayer, composed by one of our volunteers.

A PRAYER OF THE HOMELESS
(All of us)

God, my Protector, you are the MOTHER
    who nestles me under your wings . . .

You are WARMTH . . .
    rising from the subway grate
        melting my cold heart into a heart of flesh

You are the piece of BREAD on an empty stomach . . .
          received at the soup kitchen
               nourishing my famished spirit

You are WATER on parched lips . . .
          flowing from the fire hydrant
               cleansing my cluttered life

You are the gentle VOICE . . .
          a stranger who takes the time
               those I find it hard to love

But you are also my LIBERATOR from depression,
          for I call you the dream, the promise, my dignity,
               equality, enlivener, empowerer, enabler,
                    releaser from oppressive social structures.

We are all homeless, and You are our home.

Soup Kitchen Franchises

Our second soup kitchen, after the Hempstead INN, was the Long Beach Food and Friendship INN. For the first few years it operated from St. Mary's R.C. Church, but later it moved to the Martin Luther King Recreation Center. It has been going strong since October 1983.

Another soup kitchen located in Nassau is the Hicksville INN, operating in the Redeemer Lutheran Church. They have been open for more than five years and have experienced some difficulties with the local merchants who think that the facility is bringing in homeless people from other towns. This is just not so. Homeless people have been living in Hicksville for many years. I think it bothers them to see all the homeless gathered in one place at the same time. Ironically, some of the merchants who complain the loudest employ refugees, who live in Queens, at below minimum wage. These merchants themselves cause the homelessness and poverty about which they complain.

Our third soup kitchen opened in Nassau in 1986. The Freeport INN is located in the Refugee Church of Christ. This kitchen feeds 150 to 200 people daily. The United Church of Rockville Centre is a unique outreach to this facility. Every Friday the "Souper Group" meets to prepare big pots of hearty soup. When the soup is ready, the group sits down to a communal soup and bread supper. The following morning the bulk of the soup is brought to the Freeport INN. What a wonderful love-offering, this work of their hands, specially blessed by sitting together and sharing a meal in community.

Our newest Nassau soup kitchen opened in September 1989. It's our North Shore INN operating out of the First Baptist Church of Glen Cove. A very unusual impetus resulted in the opening of this site. The deputy mayor called me one day to say that the mayor was concerned that perhaps a soup kitchen or a shelter was needed in Glen Cove. What a breakthrough! This was the first time a mayor invited us in, rather than running us out of town! The mayor suggested I meet with the clergy of Glen Cove. They were most receptive to the idea and when we called our first meeting of volunteers, 150 people strong showed up. What a tribute to the compassion of the people of Glen Cove.

On the other hand, the proposed opening of a site in Far Rockaway caused a great deal of dissension. Although a grassroots group had approached us, ready and willing to open a kitchen with the support of the local clergy, other forces were at work. A small group of residents were thoroughly against the opening, and circulated petitions asking people to oppose the project. There was even a bomb scare at the site as a warning to abandon the project. Although it was never stated, the bottom line was the opposition's fear that such a facility would bring black people from surrounding areas into this all-white enclave. Had they but opened their eyes, they would have seen the poverty in their midst and realized the dire need for such a place. As I walked along the streets, the number of hungry and homeless people was astounding. I saw many senior citizens, barely able to make it from day to day. There were also large numbers of former mental patients struggling to make ends meet. By opposing the soup kitchen, residents were perpetuating the loneliness and tragic poverty of their own community members. Besides offering physical nourishment to people on the fringe, the human companionship fostered each day would boost the morale of their impoverished, solitary neighbors.

As it turned out, a new location was found in Arverne at New Beginnings Church. This new facility, the Claddagh INN, was very small—no more than twenty people could be served at one sitting, and at least sixty were showing up each day. But the cooperation of the local churches made this tiny site a special oasis of care and nourishment. It was inspiring to see the boys from St. John's Home pitch in to clean and paint and get the soup kitchen off the ground.

Our first soup kitchen in Suffolk opened in 1984 at Grace Lutheran Church in Central Islip and was called Bethany Hospitality INN. The meals are served at tables in a very narrow hallway of the church, but the incredible dedication of the volunteers makes it possible to feed sixty to eighty people each day in this difficult situation. Fara Broggelwirth, a woman who almost single-handedly ran the operation for five years, recently retired and planned to move out of state. Tragically, just before the move, she died suddenly. She is one of the unsung heroes who make The INN possible.

Also in 1984 we opened our second Suffolk soup kitchen, the Yaphank INN, far out on Long Island. This INN primarily served the public assistance recipients who were given emergency shelter in a local motel. These folks could never afford to eat decently on the meagre amount of food money supplied by the Department of Social Services. The Yaphank INN generously filled the gap for thirty to forty hungry people.

Our soup kitchen in Patchogue tells a charming tale. Joe Tafe, a man in his sixties, gathered a group of faithful volunteers and opened St. Paul's INN in 1985. He was only able to use the church's dining room on Mondays, thus their kitchen serves lunch once a week. Others in the town heard about this and knew there was a need to open a kitchen to serve hungry people the other days. Despite one pastor who was vehemently opposed and went to the mayor to try to stop the opening, the Christian Life Center INN opened in a storefront on South Main Street in Patchogue, serving lunch Tuesday through Saturday. Donations constantly come in to pay the rent for this endeavor. This only left Sunday when the hungry were not fed. The Emanuel Lutheran Church got wind of this and decided to open Emanuel's Trinity INN for Sunday dinner only. Thanks to a host of volunteers from many churches and synagogues, the hungry in Patchogue now receive a free, nutritious meal seven days a week.

Our soup kitchen in South Huntington has a very interesting story. There are two motels for emergency housing in this area where welfare clients are placed. There are nearly 100 people, including children, housed each night in these two locations. Some St. Vincent de Paul outreach workers found that the women and children were receiving a "restaurant allowance" of $2.50 per day. This meagre amount was expected to cover three meals in a restaurant, since the motels had no cooking facilities. Needless to say, the folks were eating junk food. The Department of Social Services asked The INN to set up a soup kitchen-on-wheels to provide meals for these motel dwellers.

As usual, we sent a letter to all the churches and synagogues in the area inviting them to attend an organizational meeting to plan the opening of a soup kitchen. One hundred sixty people showed up, ready and willing to put their hands to work. The first meeting was held in January 1988 and by Easter/Passover of that year, the soup kitchen was opened. It is called the Bread Of Life INN. Meals are prepared by volunteers from many different congregations each weekday at the St. Hugh of Lincoln school cafeteria kitchen. Individual meals are placed in vans in heated containers and delivered to the guests' rooms at the two motels. The nice part about this project is that the volunteers who deliver the food have established relationships with the women and children staying at the motels. They chat with them and attempt to assist them in whatever way they can from supplying clothing, to providing transportation for shopping and for medical assistance. Some great friendships are developing there between people of different classes and races. Isn't that the beginning of the Reign of God on earth?

The Shepherd's INN, Ronkonkoma, opened its doors in St. Joseph's R.C. Church in 1986. Even in this resort community there are many hungry people. The INN feeds sixty people each weekday, many of them women and children housed in the Ronkonkoma INN, a welfare motel on the Lake. Here, once again, a group of churches joined forces and created another interfaith feeding program.

That same year, 1986, saw the opening of yet another Suffolk site, the Samaritan INN. This effort was a marvelous example of interfaith effort, spearheaded by Catholics and Lutherans—a modern "reformation." St. John's Lutheran Church hosts this kitchen whose guests are mainly senior citizens.

In 1988 the Dining INN in Middle Island opened its doors in a small church on Middle Country Road. They serve lunch at noon on Monday and dinner on Wednesdays to about thirty people. Although it is a small program, they are caring for thirty people who otherwise might not have enough to eat.

Our latest soup kitchen in Suffolk opened in 1989 in the Greek Orthodox Church of the Assumption in Port Jefferson Station. Here is an interesting town. During the '60s the town was an eyesore. In the '70s and '80s it became a tourist attraction. Seeing the sleepy little harborside town, with its curio shops and boutiques, you would never imagine that people are going to bed hungry. yet the Welcome INN opened its doors and is now feeding sixty people, one night a week. This is due to the united effort of people from many religious congregations and some with no religion at all. For them, their major creed put into action is: feed the hungry.

I am sure other villages and towns will be approaching The INN to assist them in setting up a soup kitchen. Just recently the Babylon clergy appointed a committee to study the problem in their area. The INN is working with this group, exploring the possibility of another soup kitchen-on-wheels program to a welfare motel in the area.

Little Miracles

This work is surely a work of God. It would never have grown as rapidly as it has, with so little money and a non-paid staff, if it were not of God. There are many stories of "little miracles" at our soup kitchens. One of these "miracles" happened in Hempstead when the line of guests was longer than the stew pot was deep. The volunteers had literally dished out the last portion and were frantic as to how to feed the fifty people still on line. At that very moment, through the door came people from a local church who were delivering leftover sandwiches and salads from a church luncheon.

Thank you God, for the manna from heaven, for the loaves and fishes, for honoring your promise that the hungry will be fed. Truly you are a God of the poor.

INN, Inc.

What does it mean for a soup kitchen to come under the umbrella of The INN? What are The INN's responsibilities to the new group and vice versa?

The INN, for its part, promises to allow the new group to come under its incorporation. Thus the new kitchen can use our tax exempt number when purchasing food, supplies and equipment. Whenever The INN writes a grant which could apply to our satellites, the new kitchen would be included. In publicizing our work, all our branches are mentioned. Since there is strength in numbers, the larger we grow the better chance we will have of changing some of the unjust systems which cause poverty. An elected official (and grantors for that matter) will be more inclined to listen to an agency representing 16 soup kitchens than to a single soup kitchen. The INN networks food from one kitchen to another, when one has a superabundance of one commodity and another's cupboards are bare. Also, when a big donation of food comes our way, we notify all our satellites, and they pick up what they need. We also purchase food in bulk for our kitchens, so we can get a better price than if each location were to bargain individually.

The responsibilities of the new kitchen involve their willingness to include the word "INN" with their title. This officially and legally, but especially spiritually, links it to our agency. The branches are asked to refer to The INN whenever they do public relations and agree to share any surplus food or money they receive with the poorer, less fortunate branches of The INN. The local branch must pay half the insurance cost each year, with the main office picking up the rest.

Overall, this relationship has been mutually advantageous and morally uplifting. When we tell our audiences that our soup kitchens feed over 1,200 people each day, with the assistance of volunteers, they are astounded. This year, for the first time, we hosted a "thank you" party for all 1,100 INN volunteers. The spirit was electric. Imagine bringing together in one spot over 1,100 people who rub shoulders regularly with God's favorites. These are today's living saints.

We find such wonderful love and sharing among people in our soup kitchens. Rich people mingle with poor people and many stories of life are shared. Some interesting results have occurred.

Jean and Rob

This story dates back to the early planing stages of our first soup kitchen, the Hempstead INN. Jean chaired our Volunteer Committee. Rob was one of the potential volunteers.

At the end of a planning meeting at Hofstra, as the two were leaving the room, I noticed a special glance between them. I said to Pat O'Connor (co-founder and mother of nine), "I think something is going on between Rob and Jean."

"Nonsense," she replied, "how would you know, you unromantic old man? I'm married with nine kids. I would know if something were brewing long before you."

Six months later, as Rob and Jean were announcing their engagement, Pat sheepishly apologized. I never let her forget her rash and inaccurate comment. As Rob and Jean were presented with a soup tureen as a wedding gift, I winked at Pat across the table!

Irma

Another touching event occurred on Thanksgiving Day 1985. Irma was a regular at our Hempstead INN. She was about 68 years old and walked quite a distance each day to the soup kitchen. She was a very stately, graceful woman who appeared to be visiting the President as she waited on line at the soup kitchen. She had such elegance about her. Irma seldom spoke, but on Thanksgiving Day that year, as we were cutting up twenty turkeys and were inundated with more volunteers than we could use, she made her way through the crowd and handed me a piece of paper. She said, "I just want you to know how much I appreciate eating here each day. It's the only decent meal I eat. Here's a poem I wrote to show how much this place means to me."

I opened the folded piece of looseleaf paper and read this beautiful poem:

THANKSGIVING

I am giving thanks to you dear God,
For all you have done for me,
For helping me bear these burdens in life,
And for blessings that are yet to be.

I want to thank you for my daily bread,
The sunshine and the rain,
For knowing my humble prayers,
that make me smile again.

I want to thank you for the gift of life,
In which I learned to care,
To always lend a helping hand,
to a stranger or a friend.

It's nice to know that you are there,
Whenever dark shadows come our way,
We know that we are fully blessed in sharing
with you this beautiful Thanksgiving day.

Andy

Another poem was written by a very special man, Andy, who is a carpenter by trade. His energetic work for The INN is intense, as is his spiritual depth. He has never taken a penny for the hundreds of hours he has spent helping to renovate houses which we use as shelters.

At the dedication of the Bread of Life INN in South Huntington, where meals are brought to welfare motels, he asked if he could read a poem he wrote. We were all moved as he read these lines, with a gentleness and sincerity so characteristic of him.

GIFT OF LOVE

Hand to unseen hand,
heart to unseen heart,
love to unseen love.

Till the giver and the receiver
see again that they are
One people
One body
One hunger
One and only one real gift
To give to each other.

And so let us begin here tonight.

To peel and to dice,
to butter and to boil,
To package and to send out
ourselves in disguise
In the knowledge that those
Who may not see us or know us,
Will taste a sweetness beyond the bread.

Michael

Finally, we come to Michael, a poet and regular at the Hempstead INN. He was a young man with an emotional problem which was leading him into drugs. When he was good, he was very, very good. When he was bad, he was horrid. Our volunteers deserve gold medals for their enduring patience with Michael.

One day, as we were preparing for our "Have a Heart for the Homeless Candlelight Vigil" at the United Way in Melville, Michael asked if he could read one of his poems there. With fear and trepidation, we said yes.

On February 14, 1989, one thousand people gathered, ready to stand up and say to our elected officials, "We need housing for poor people on Long Island." Michael made his way to the podium. With full T.V., radio and newspaper coverage, I held my breath as he began to read, praying that it would be appropriate.

"O, ye of little faith," I said to myself, as all 1,000 people listened in awed silence to his touching poem. I share part of it with you below.

ONLY THE HOMELESS

Only the homeless, once upon a time
was me,
Only the homeless—there are so many you see.
Every day is sadness,
Filled with cruelty, drugs, and all types of badness.
They no longer know gladness.
Not knowing where they will stay day after day.
Their meals, they sometimes steal,
Sad, but real.

Only the homeless—don't know what
it is to be free.
For they are bound to the land,
with no door, no key.
What brought them here, nobody
knows,
but their number grows and grows.
Can you imagine a child,
Getting eaten up by human
crocodiles,
Or old folks treated like jokes
by uncompassionate folks,
Who look to poke fun at them . . .

Only the homeless have filled their
breast
With heartache and pain.
Lord knows how they keep from going
insane.
It's a mystery to me
But it is made clear, this is not
going to disappear . . .

As babies cry
And mothers sigh,

Because they can't satisfy
The hunger felt.
My, but this is so real.

Only the homeless
The children of the restless,
Caught up in this mess,
Only the homeless go on forever —
Only the homeless
God blesses you all!

Coming Home

I want to conclude this chapter by bringing us back to a scene I left unfinished. As we packed up our things that sad day in Hempstead, having been evicted from our third and final church, we promised our 150 guests that one day we would return to them. We were forced to move our operation to Freeport, but we knew one day we would come back. We had to come back.

We knew that none of the churches in Hempstead would have us. The only solution was to buy our own building; that way we couldn't be evicted. Well, where were we to get the money to do such a thing?

I went to visit the local parish in Garden City, St. Joseph's. I told the pastor, Father Emil Wcela (now Bishop), of our great desire to return to Hempstead and of my plan to purchase a building—a home of our own for The INN. I asked him for the names of some parishioners whom I might approach for donations.

He thought for a while, and then said, "First of all, I want to help. I'll pledge $16,000 from St. Joseph's towards the purchase of such a facility. I know the terrible problem of poverty in Hempstead. This is the least we can do."

"Secondly," he said, "let me think of which parishioners we could approach."

A week later he called me to say that the Bishop had been in touch with him asking for names of parishioners who could contribute to the annual Bishop's Appeal. Father Wcela said he was sorry, but he could only offer me one name, John Brennan. One week later, Father

Wcela called to tell me that Mr. Brennan was open to the idea of speaking with me and that I could contact him.

I met John Brennan at his home in Garden City. He had heard a little about The INN, and had lots of questions about our work. He shared with me his distaste for bureaucracy, "You know," he said, "I never contribute to big institutions. Too much goes into administrative costs. I much prefer to contribute to groups like yours where I know most of my money will go into direct service." Then came the shocker. "I can help you," said Mr. Brennan. "We'll begin with a donation of stock worth about $60,000." I sat there in shock. I had only met the man one hour ago and yet he was willing to take a risk and assist us in purchasing our own building. Over the next year, Mr. Brennan contributed $150,000 to The INN.

With money in hand, I went searching for our new location. How lucky I was to find a building on Front Street in Hempstead. It had a large space on the ground floor for our soup kitchen and plenty of room upstairs for our offices and later a thrift shop, which operated for one year and later moved to a local church under its sponsorship. At the thrift shop we "sold" at very low cost or gave away clothing to the people who eat at our soup kitchen. We charged ten cents, twenty-five cents, fifty cents for the clothing which was donated to us. We asked our guests for a small donation so as to preserve their own dignity. It wasn't a handout. Also, by contributing this small amount, they knew they were assisting in the work of feeding the hungry in Hempstead.

We had the building under contract, and now it was time to announce to the mayor that we were returning to Hempstead. By that time, our soup kitchen in Freeport had enough local volunteers to continue feeding up to 200 people each weekday.

I called the mayor's office. "Mayor," I said, "The INN has purchased a building on Front Street and we are returning to Hempstead."

"Oh no," he blurted, "I thought when you went to Freeport that was the end of you. You know I got a lot of flack from my constituents because of your presence here. Don't even think about returning."

What was I to do? Here we had a site and lots of

hungry people, but bureaucracy was threatening to stand in the way.

"I know what I'll do," I said to myself. "There's a lot of power in the Church, and we must use this power for the sake of the people."

I paid a visit to the mayor's pastor. "Reverend," I began, "you were a great supporter of The INN when we were in Hempstead."

"Yes," he said, "what a shame you had to leave town. There are still so many hungry and homeless people here."

"Well, we want to come back. As a matter of fact, a generous donor has given us the money to buy a building so we can't get evicted anymore."

"Wonderful!" the pastor said.

"But the mayor says we're not welcome. He claims that the village doesn't want us back. I'm afraid he can put many blocks in our way."

"Well," the pastor said, "you know the mayor is one of my parishioners."

"Yes, I know that."

He picked up the phone and dialed the mayor's office. "Mayor," he began, "did you hear the The INN is returning to Hempstead?"

"Don't worry, Pastor," said the mayor, "I have the situation under control. They won't get back into town."

"Nonsense," the pastor retorted, "there's a tremendous need here for The INN. They must come back. As a matter of fact, our church will be co-sponsoring the soup kitchen along with The INN."

There was a long pause at the other end of the line. "Yes, pastor, as you wish," came the reply. And that was that! The power of the church acted on behalf of the poor and the victory was ours. Alleluia! We would return. The hungry would be fed. God's work would be done.

On a beautiful afternoon in May 1986, we dedicated "The Mary Brennan INN." The soup kitchen was packed with over 100 people. John Brennan spoke of his mother, for whom the soup kitchen was named. A rabbi, priest, and our friend, the mayor's pastor, prayed in earnest that the hungry would be fed and that God's favorites would be cared for. We sang, prayed, laughed and celebrated. Some of our guests were there, wearing jubilant smiles.

We played a tape of Vivaldi's triumphal music—yes, we were returning to Hempstead in glory!

At the last minute, a car pulled up and the mayor stepped out. The place became very still. He walked in, came to the front of the room and very solemnly said, "Mr. Moran thinks I don't want you here. But I want you to know you are welcome. I want to present this official citation to The INN, in appreciation for the work you have done and will do here in Hempstead to feed the hungry. I never realized how many hungry people there are in Hempstead."

The mayor received a standing ovation. God be praised! Conversions are possible! The "powers that be" really can be moved. The system can be changed. All it takes is prayer (lots of it) and a friendly nudge from the Church! We are back in Hempstead. Amen. Alleluia!

Chapter 3

A Place to
Lay Their Heads

We kept meeting people at the soup kitchen who had no place to call home. We would offer them a bag of groceries, and they would say, "Thanks, but I don't have a home. Sometimes I live in a car or an abandoned building." Or they might reply: "I only have a single room with no kitchen facilities. I'm not even allowed to have a hotplate. Just let me have what I can eat from a can." Others told us horror stories of living in a boarding house which had turned into a crack den or of living in someone's dormitory-style basement or living room, with ten cots lined up one next to the other. By charging each person $200 a month, unscrupulous landlords were making a bundle. One of the worst stories was about a landlord who was renting out rooms on an eight-hour-a-day basis. This way he could have three shifts over a twenty-four hour period! Isn't this truly an immoral way of making money off poor people?

We knew we had to do something about this. We needed to provide a place of hospitality for these fringe folks who often ended up being evicted and having to live with relatives, friends, or even sleep in parks and train stations.

In 1984 we opened our first overnight shelter for homeless people. We named it Hospitality INN.

The concept took about one year in planning. First of all, we knew that we didn't want to repeat the mistakes made in New York City where armories served as shelters. Sometimes hundreds of cots would line the room like gravestones. Then people wondered why these shelters were places of violence and neglect. If you herd the homeless together like cattle and treat them like dirt, that's precisely the way they respond—to one another, the staff and towards themselves. We knew we needed to provide a clean place where they could be treated with respect and where they could rediscover their own worth and dignity. You can't do that in a barracks. We knew that if we were to provide a house of hospitality, it had to be done on a small scale, and it had to feel like home.

We found such a place at the Campus Parish House near Hofstra University. The Roman Catholic Diocese of Rockville Centre owned a house in a racially integrated neighborhood where the college chaplains resided. Since I was still a chaplain at Hofstra, I went to the Diocese and asked if we could use the house as a shelter for the homeless. The Diocesan Administrator at the time, Joseph Barbero, was a man of deep compassion. He had worked in social services for many years and was keenly aware of the plight of poor people on Long Island. He went to work, cut through all the red tape, and within a few months, we had permission to use the house to shelter the homeless. The Veatch Program of the Unitarian Universalist Church gave us $25,000 to add a living room, bathroom, three bedrooms and an office during the summer of 1984.

The house was in place, but what were we do about the staff? There was a model in Brooklyn which seemed to fit the bill. A visionary named Sister Elaine Roulet had established a series of Providence Houses—places of hospitality for homeless women and children. Some of the Sisters living in these houses were willing to assist me in applying the concepts of their model to Long Island.

The most unique feature of their houses was the presence of a live-in community. Four to seven people volunteered one year to form a family-like community in each house. It was similar to the Peace Corps concept, except here each person paid $250 a month towards room and board as a way of personally supporting the work. In addition to working full time outside, they took turns being "on duty" at the house week nights and weekends. "Duty" meant being responsible for the smooth functioning of the house: seeing to the evening meal preparation, serving, cleanup, attending to the needs of the homeless guests, providing an orientation and completing an intake sheet on new guests, answering the door and telephone, etc. The community realized that their ministry could only be accomplished in a prayerful and supportive atmosphere so they promised to pray together every day. By forming a close-knit community of care and concern, they could extend warm, family-like hospitality to homeless guests.

Where could we find such dedicated people for our house? I thought immediately of a Sister friend working in Appalachia who was looking to relocate to Long Island.

I wrote to her: "Dear Aurelie, The INN is opening a shelter for the homeless. We need community members. I think God is calling you to this work."

She wrote back: "Dear Michael, I'm 62 years old. The Daughters of Wisdom would never let me live in with the homeless, nor would they allow me to join a mixed community of men and women. But, may God's will be done."

Three months later she wrote that she was moving in!

Steve and Felix, who had been members of the Hofstra Catholic Parish, heard about this new venture and asked if they could be part of it. Finally, we recruited a former Sister who was now living with her family. We discovered that many young people in their twenties and thirties are drawn to ministry but don't want the permanent commitment of the religious life. A short-term commitment to the homeless with a community support system appeals to them. The INN took advantage of this attraction.

I realized that asking people to join the new community was not enough. I was being called to join them. Living with the homeless would be an exciting challenge. I knew I could give a lot; little did I realize how much I'd get from the experience.

Over the first April weekend in 1984, five candidates for the community gathered to do some strategic planning and to test out our ability to live together. We were assisted by two Sisters from Providence House, Mary Dunleavy and Maryellen Kane, who helped us apply their model of hospitality to The INN.

Finally, the moment of signing the dotted line came, and the Spirit of Humor enlightened us. "Today is April Fool's Day," commented Aurelie, "what a perfect day to be fools for Yahweh and put ourselves and this project in God's hands." We all laughed and one by one signed the agreement to live together for one year in prayerful community—sharing our home with those who had none. It was a sacred moment.

Word spread quickly about our new home. People started delivering furniture, curtains, kitchen utensils, dinnerware, etc. I'll never forget finding the garage filled with donations! It took the entire weekend to sort everything out on the front lawn. Our neighbors came by thinking we were having a garage sale!

Since each member of the community had a full daytime job it was necessary to hire a coordinator to attend to the guests and the house during the day. The person needed to be a Jack/Jill of all trades—someone who could deal in a kind, practical way with the guests, motivating them to seek out permanent housing, social services, and medical care. This coordinator would also need to supervise the volunteers, keep the house in shape and food on the table. Quite a comprehensive job description! Where on earth was The INN to find a person to fill this role?

During the summer we searched high and low for a coordinator. We finally found such a graced individual in the person of Sister Pat Kollmer. She had been a teacher and spiritual director of young adults, but she felt in her bones that now was the time to work with poor people. She was the perfect angel: hyperactive, dedicated, excellent with people (although her loud laugh could drive you crazy) and very practical. Just the person we needed.

Finally, with the new extension completed, all rooms freshly painted and furnished, the day coordinator and community in place, we took occupancy of Hospitality INN on September 1, 1984. We were ready to begin our new ministry of providing hospitality to homeless people.

One of our first guests was a single mother with five children! They had been evicted by a landlord who decided he didn't want all those children in his house. This family set the stage for the guests we would welcome into Hospitality INN. Originally we anticipated that most of our guests would be street people. What a shock it was to find that the people sent to us were mostly the new poor—people who had been able to hang on by their fingertips but were now falling through the governmental safety nets. Our guests included abused women and their children, runaway and throwaway teenagers, senior citizens whose children didn't want them anymore, people released from alcohol and drug rehabilitation programs, working poor who couldn't afford their own place, and people evicted from their homes. They all ended up with us! They were referred by the Department of Social Services, private social service agencies and church pastors. They remained with us two to four weeks depending on their motivation and ability to help themselves. During their stay we would assist them in finding a permanent place to live and connect them to counseling and medical services.

Soon we had to turn people away because the house was filled. We were horrified by the large numbers of homeless people and the terrible lack of facilities to assist them.

All of this would have been overwhelming if it were not for the support of one another in community, a real bonding with our guests and seeing small successes. As we came into daily contact with human tragedies, we needed to be surrounded with a cape of humor or it and we would have fallen apart.

One humorous story that carried us through occurred during our first month of operation. A new family had arrived one night after I had retired to my room. The next morning while I was in the bathroom, a knock came at the door. I heard the ten-year-old voice of Laura moaning: "White man, when you gonna get out of that bathroom?" I was completely thrown off guard. Through the closed door, I shouted back, "First of all, my name's not 'white man' it's Michael. And second, I'll be out in ten minutes." That evening at supper I told the story to our guests and the community. We all laughed and enjoyed this strange and new adventure—people of different races and backgrounds living together peacefully under one roof.

The next morning I had my chance to get even. Laura beat me to the bathroom. I knocked on the door and shouted: "Black girl, when you gonna get out of that bathroom?" "Very funny!" came the reply.

We learned early on that without humor, the project would have died an early death.

Another incident we still chuckle about involved our pay phone. We had a semi-public pay phone installed so that our guests, including children, would be able to make and receive phone calls. The phone number we were given had formerly been assigned to our local Waldbaum's supermarket.

Often the phone would ring and the caller would ask, "What time are you open until tonight?" or "Are you having a sale on chopped meat?" We'd laugh off these annoying interruptions, but Sister Aurelie would get frustrated and bark at all of us every time she took one of these calls.

One day I decided to play a joke on her so I called the pay phone from my office. "Hello," Sister Aurelie began.

"This is Waldbaum's. Do you have any messages?" I said.

"Messages," she shouted "we are sick and tired of getting your calls. We don't know your sale prices and don't care to give out that information."

"I'm terribly sorry but would you be interested in making a little extra money by being our answering service?"

Aurelie was furious, "Absolutely not. We are busy enough around here without answering your calls. How dare you even ask!"

I started laughing and gave myself away.

"I hate you, Michael!" she cried as she hung up the phone!

Our guests are a unique group: all ages and races, from different backgrounds and classes. The amazing thing is that they care for one another. One person in crisis reaches out to calm another and lend an open ear.

When our guests arrive there is a mixed reaction. They are nervous and scared to be in a shelter. But at the same time they look around and see how clean and neat the house is and how people are getting along and we see a slight relaxation in their faces. In a few days, guests who arrived angry and uptight, relax and join in the family-like atmosphere, doing household chores and treating one another as old friends.

I remember when Joan got upset when another guest corrected her son. Joan shouted, "Don't you reprimand my child."

Mary, who had been at the shelter for three weeks, calmly responded, "You're new here. You don't understand this place. We care for one another and watch out for each other's kids. That's what makes this such a special place." That stopped Joan in her tracks and the very next day I saw her feeding someone else's baby.

A touching incident occurred during the first few months of operation. Vera had been abused by her husband and was slowly putting the pieces of her life back together. Angela arrived at our house, distraught because her husband had come home drunk, beat up her and her two children, and thrown them out of the house. Vera stayed up until two a.m. listening to Angela's story and relating her own trials and tribulations. Angela finally calmed down and slept like a baby. Our guests minister to one another and help in the healing process far more effectively than anyone on our staff.

Needless to say, it is embarrassing for our guests to tell their relatives and friends that they are staying in a shelter. They'll often say they are staying with a friend or renting a room in a boarding house.

A young guest, Tom, made friends with some local teenagers. One day he was talking with them outside our house, when Sister Aurelie drove up. He ran over to her and kissed her saying, "Hi, Grandma." Later he came into the house and approached Aurelie. "I'm sorry for embarrassing you outside, Sister, but I don't want my friends to know I'm staying in a shelter. I told them I was visiting my grandmother."

"No problem," replied Aurelie, "I'm happy to be your adopted grandma." At that, they gave each other a big, familial hug.

Some of our guests become so much a part of the family that they believe it is their home. One evening a live-in community member, Carol, was talking with Sue, a six-year-old guest. They were playing a game and Carol said, "Let's tell about our homes. I live in a big white house."

"I live in a big white house too."

"My house is filled with many loving people and has a lot of rooms."

Sue repeated the same. As they continued, it became obvious that Sue truly considered the shelter her home.

Family spirit is evident when I look around the dining room table at the black and white and Asian faces. It is like a United Nations meeting. It occurs to me that this is perhaps the first time for some of our guests to share something as sacred as a family meal with people of different races. How wonderful the world would be if each of us could sit down at table with people of different races, classes, nationalities and religions to eat and talk and laugh together as one family.

I know our guests will carry with them and tell others: "We all ate together—black and Chinese and white—you know something, we acted as a family, not as strangers."

It's amazing that some of our guests ever arrive at the door. Often a worker at the Department of Social Services, in an attempt to save the taxpayers' money, will try to discourage a guest from coming to our house since the Department pays us on a per diem basis. The worker will say something like, "Do you really want to go to a shelter where the nuns run a strict house like a convent?"

We have successes and failures with our guests. Take for example, Ray and Jose. They came to us on the same day from New Hope, an alcohol-detox program. They were waiting for room at a residential rehabilitation program. Existing programs are booked to capacity and if you don't have insurance you can wait forever.

Their families wouldn't take them back so we took on the supportive role of a family. Both Ray and Jose went out each day to Tempforce and took part-time jobs to save money for their own rooms once they finished rehabilitation.

Then came Ray's 30th birthday. Missing the curfew, he arrived at midnight in a state of drunkenness. Jose and I helped him to his room and I could see tears welling up in Jose's eyes. He kept saying, "Please give Ray another chance. It's his birthday. He slipped."

We did give him another chance, but the following Friday night he fell a second time. We couldn't allow him to stay, especially with a household of people who were obeying the rules and some who had come from abusive alcoholic situations. Jose embraced Ray as he left to go.

That night in our community room we paused to pray. We felt like such failures yet we knew we had done all we could. We offered an atmosphere of loving support. It was up to Ray to respond and to change himself.

The following week Jose was accepted to the Plainview Rehab Program. As I drove him there I saw the sadness in his eyes—he was only half, not whole. He had made it but his dear friend, Ray, was lost somewhere in his own nightmare.

Dorothy Day House

In 1985 I saw a TV movie entitled *An Early Frost*. It was about a young man who struggled with and finally died of AIDS. I knew immediately that The INN needed to respond to the growing number of homeless people with AIDS. So many were being rejected by family and friends, left to die alone, sometimes on the streets. The INN needed to open up a shelter where they could live and die in peace in a loving atmosphere.

The INN Board struggled with their decision to open a shelter for PWA's (Persons with AIDS). The need was there, but could The INN sustain the negative reaction of the public to such a project? At that time, the majority of PWA's were gay and a frequent twisted reaction of the heterosexual community was, "They deserve what they got. It's God's way of punishing them. The world can do without them."

This attitude is completely unfounded in both the Jewish and Christian scriptures. Yahweh is always depicted as the defender of the abandoned. Those rejected by society are the most tenderly cared for by the God of the Hebrew scriptures and by Jesus in the Christian scriptures.

As the Christians on the Board worried about being thrown to the lions for opening such a shelter, two Jewish Board members said: "Of course it's a risk, but what else can we do? The need is there. These are among the most vulnerable of our homeless people today. If we are to be true to our mission, we can't turn our backs on them. We must open up." The vote to open was unanimous!

We found a large house in the Town of Hempstead which was available for lease. On one weekend 45 volunteers did all the painting and repairs necessary to change the place from an eyesore to a treasured home. Furniture was donated and curtains were hung on every window.

We opened on March 2, 1986 after only two months of preparation. We called the house the Dorothy Day House in honor of that brave woman who founded the Catholic Worker Movement. She was the first to take people off the streets into shelters during the years following the Great Depression. Her patience and openness to all, especially society's rejects, made her a fit patron for the difficult work we were about to undertake.

When we opened our doors to our first residents, our capacity was six guests. During its operation, 23 PWA's lived with dignity and died in peace in this special place.

A most incredible, dedicated and over-worked staff maintained this facility. They were overwhelmed by the needs and demands but with the help of many volunteers, our staff struggled to serve our guests lovingly on their journey to death.

There were unique stories of spiritual awakening and acceptance of death at Dorothy Day House. There were reunions of families and friends who had ostracized their loved ones. There were nights of excruciating pain, terror, loneliness and lots of hand-holding of guests by staff and volunteers.

At Dorothy Day House, one never had to face death alone. Those who had been abandoned, condemned and cast aside were embraced by a community who reached out with God's love.

Tim

Tim came to Dorothy Day a young, defeated man recently diagnosed with full-blown AIDS. His family and friends had rejected him. Tim was bitter and hate-filled, resisting the idea of death but utterly fed up with life. Tim was the first guest Sister Aurelie, our coordinator, received into the house. "For four months he wouldn't even talk to me," she remembered. "He'd have nothing to do with me, especially since I was a nun. In his rage against a God who was allowing him to die, he took out his hostility on me in a passive-aggressive way. I was afraid of him and just let him have his space."

Then came the turning point. "One day I converted

him," Aurelie recalled, "not with prayer but with oatmeal!" She continued with a twinkle in her eye, "it was a cold January morning and Tim was exhausted after a night filled with sweating, diarrhea and tears. He came to the breakfast table and I served him piping-hot oatmeal. He looked at me and simply said, 'Thank you.' That's what ended the cold war. After that we were on speaking terms."

Although Tim had been raised in a religious household, he had abandoned his faith. His disease just confirmed in his mind that a loving God could never exist. Slowly he began asking Sister Aurelie questions about religion and God. When she told him she was a celibate religious he exclaimed, "How have you lived all these years without a man?"

"Well, now I have you," Aurelie replied. And Tim smiled in thanks.

A few weeks before he died, Tim attended Mass in the house, and joined in willingly at the dialogue homily, sharing that he had resolved his lifelong battle with God.

The day before he died, Sister Aurelie had a visit from her Superior General and some other Sisters. She brought them to Tim's room for a visit. (Several of the nuns later said that they were scared to death!) As they were leaving his room, Tim whispered, "God bless you." And indeed, God had blessed them because in only a few hours Tim would be with God.

The irony of The INN is the convergence of roles. The saint and sinner meet, the church-goer is blessed by the gay man with AIDS, the homeless joins the volunteers for prayer, the wealthy doctor sits down to a meal with a drug addict. And no one judges the other. The saint could be the real sinner and the sinner could be the real saint. But it doesn't really matter when you are sitting face to face across the dinner table.

PWA's

In 1988 some difficulties arose in our shelter for PWA's and we were forced to close Dorothy Day House in June. We promised ourselves that if it were possible we would open again. The number of AIDS victims has grown and although there seems to be more interest in caring for them, many are still rejected and find themselves homeless. If we are to be true to our mission, The INN must find ways of sheltering these vulnerable souls.

A new shelter for PWA's will open in 1990. Although we can rely upon the dedication and goodwill of volunteers, we must have a sterling and full-time staff in place to care adequately for the eight beautiful people who will reside in our newest shelter, The Anne Frank INN. We have chosen that name because of the similarity between this heroic woman and our guests. She was hidden away, rejected, scared and lonely. Yet her autobiography is clear on one thing: she never lost hope. With God's help, and with a dedicated staff and volunteers, our guests won't lose hope either.

Oscar Romero Inn

In 1987 we opened the Oscar Romero INN, named after the Archbishop of San Salvador who surrendered a wealthy lifestyle, to defend the rights of poor people against a government which served only the rich. One day, as he celebrated Mass, he was shot to death by those who disapproved of his actions.

The people who live in this INN are truly homeless. They had to leave their native land of Central America and come to a nation which doesn't want them. Their problems in learning our language and in securing jobs are tremendous. They are refugees but our nation will not accept them. They truly are people without a home.

This INN is most unique. American volunteers live side by side with their Spanish-speaking sisters and brothers. We are learning to live together in peace and respect for our differences and in celebration of our many likenesses.

Angela Merici INN

In 1987 we also opened the Angela Merici INN, our only shelter in Suffolk County. Five Sisters from different religious congregations live in community and offer hospitality to homeless single women and their children. Since our coordinator and several community members speak Spanish, we are able to accept guests who only speak Spanish.

Some off our best coordinators are women who have raised children and know the ins and outs of practical household management. Like Josephine Nuevo, who is originally from Cuba.

I'll never forget opening day at Angela Merici. Josephine was busy and nervous with a hundred last minute tasks. In order to add a little lightness to the serious occasion, and because I can never resist playing a practical joke, I telephoned her. "Mrs. Nuevo, I'm a counselor with a local agency and I understand that you have opened up a shelter for the homeless."

"Yes," she said proudly.

"Well, I believe I have some customers for you."

"Yes, of course," replied the anxious but welcoming Josephine, "We have plenty of room."

"That's splendid. I have a homeless family, mother, father and ten children."

There was a pregnant pause. "Ten children?" she asked in amazement.

"Yes," I said, "ten children."

"Oh my God," she blurted out, "that's all my beds."

"Splendid," I concluded, "I'm sending them right over."

"Wait, wait, wait," she shouted, at which I burst into a fit of laughter. She recognized my laugh and said, "Mike Moran, you are a bad man!"

Rosa Parks INN

In December of 1986 we purchased a legal boarding house in Roosevelt. Despite unsafe and unsanitary conditions, the former landlord had managed to squeeze high rents from his tenants. For two years we struggled, with the assistance of over 100 volunteers, to transform this hovel into a beautiful home.

We decided to open a transitional shelter for homeless families there, especially for single women and their children. We know the difficulties faced by poor single mothers, especially those who are black. In the Rosa Parks INN, guests stay with us for as long as six months.

We chose the name Rosa Parks INN in honor of that

brave woman who sat so defiantly in the white section of the bus in Alabama in 1955. She was a hard working, low-salaried black laborer who was just plain tired from her job and from being pushed around and walked over by a racist society. She was pooped, and she just wouldn't give up that seat! She was arrested; people came to her defense and a movement towards equal rights was born.

Times change but the evils of classism, sexism and racism remain with us, often more dangerously subtle than overt. We wanted to provide an oasis from this madness where the women could claim their own power and plan new directions. We help the women to discover their own gifts and talents. They are exposed to group work and seminars which focus on topics such as "How to Prevent Children's Protective Services from Taking Your Kids Away from You" (also known as "Good Child Rearing Practices"); "How to Deal with Your Landlord/Landlady" (for "Public Relations, Interpersonal Skills and Assertiveness Training"); "How To Still Have Money at the End of the Month" (translated "Household Management and Budgeting"); "Keeping Your Body Beautiful" (also known as "Nutrition and Exercise") and "How to Leave Poverty Behind" (or "Information and Counseling on Education and Career Choices, Job Training, Preparing for a Job Interview").

The hope is that these seminars will assist our women to be independent once they settle into permanent housing (if they can find affordable housing). The most popular groups by far are those conducted by women who have walked in their shoes and are now doing well on their own. There is a depth of sharing which helps the women see themselves as they really are, without masks, and assists them in developing a healthy self-respect and genuine dignity. They learn so gracefully from one another.

Dorothy Day INN

In the meantime, the house we had used for persons with AIDS was reopened as a shelter for homeless families and singles and is now the Dorothy Day INN.

Like some of our other shelters, three or four people live in community and provide a home-like atmosphere for our guests. We also have a dedicated staff of two coordinators who split the work day into two shifts.

If the walls in this house could talk, you'd hear some wonderful stories. For example, one evening Louise, a community member, recruited our young guests to write to a young African boy. She instructed them as she distributed paper and pen to each child. "OK," she said "tell him about yourself and what it's like living here at Dorothy Day INN."

The youthful hands turned into a sea of written movement. "There wasn't a sound, recalled Louise. "You could hear a pin drop. They were all so attentive to this important task." Then she paused and said, "You know, it reminded me of what the world should be about. People reaching out to people—across the globe—minimizing differences, celebrating cultural diversity and similarities that span nations and races. In this wonderful INN the children were teaching the adults how to be peacemakers."

This lesson so impressed Louise that several nights later she had a dream. When she wrote down the dream, being as true to details as she could remember. Here is what she wrote:

Flight into the Future

Dreams can be very real and they can come true. I had a beautiful dream that is truly a flight into the future. I will share it with you, and hope all our good dreams come true.

I found myself on an airplane landing in Canada. I entered the airport and noticed people from all over the world: men, women and children, all colors and speaking all different languages, wearing beautiful and unusual costumes from their countries. They all seemed to be walking around freely, everyone being welcomed and greeted.

I looked around for signs to tell me where Customs was, but there weren't any. I asked someone, "Excuse me, where is Customs?"

The person said, "Customs?"

I said, "Yes, you know, when people come from different countries..."

"Yes, every country and people have their own customs."

"No," I said, "don't you have to check through Customs?"

The person looked puzzled. Suddenly he said, "Oh, that kind of Customs! We haven't had that since the world declared peace."

"The world declared peace!" I exclaimed in delight.

The people all turned around and said, "Yes!"

Then I noticed in the distance that there were clowns and mimes and dancers and jugglers and magicians. I said, "Is there something special going on?"

"No, they're always here, ever since the world declared joy."

I said, "The world declared joy!"

Again the people turned around and joyfully exclaimed, "Yes!"

I decided to hurry up and see what else was new in the outside world. This had not been some ordinary journey. Somehow, I had arrived in the future.

I asked my new friend, "Is there a place around here where I can change my money? All I have is American money."

He said, "Money? We don't use money anymore."

"Then what do you do if you want something?" I asked. I couldn't wait to hear.

"You ask for it. If anyone in the world needs something that anyone else has, they share it."

"How long has this been going on?"

"Since the world declared love."

"The world declared love!" I shouted.

"Yes!" those around me shouted.

"So there are no more starving children? And what about disease? And people can travel whenever and wherever they want?" The questions came pouring out of me.

Suddenly I understood. With no threat of war, all effort that had been expended for war and defense went into peace, joy and love.

"And these people from all over the world, are they always here, too?" I asked.

"No. They've all come to Canada for the yearly worship. Canada was chosen this year, and these people are coming to share their own way of worshipping God. They aren't priests or government officials, they're just ordinary people coming to share their gifts and themselves because it's their turn."

"Once we were no longer protecting what we owned, we were able to share our faith and ideas about God and religion. We realized that there is only one God, but many ways of expressing our love and relationship with that God. We saw that one was not right and the other wrong, just different, and each one beautiful. So once a year, representatives from every group come together to celebrate our being one world, under God, indivisible, with peace, joy and love for all."

Those around us had stopped to listen to a story which was familiar to them.

Together they joined in a joyful and resounding "YES!"

Rene

Not all the stories have such a pleasant ending. The community and staff at Dorothy Day INN vividly recall Rene and her six children.

Rene was a single parent who was more interested in disciplining her children than loving them. They ranged in age from three to sixteen. When they first arrived, our daytime coordinator, Judy, greeted them and showed them the three rooms she had reserved for their large family. "No," Rene snapped, "we'll all sleep together in one room."

During their stay with us, whenever Judy or a volunteer would take a child on his or her lap, Rene would yell at the child. When they'd leave for the day, Rene would take one sandwich for the whole family. The tragic part was when Judy tried to talk with Rene in the office, "All Rene would do in her brokenness was cry and cry and cry, tears she could never show her kids. She felt like such a failure as a mother and a person," said Judy sadly.

We have a lot of Renes. Girls who become women too quickly. Children having children. Lost, bewildered, frightened. Trying to make it alone, they are deathly afraid the "authorities" will take away their children— their only real possessions. And they struggle along, despite all their obstacles and inadequacies, not to mention that accusing finger of people who say, "Well why did she have so many children? It's her own fault."

If only we could walk in another's shoes for a while. Why can't we ever understand the tragic and tender lives of those around us and how life's experiences leave such indelible marks on us. Lord, that I may see!

Nancy

Rene's story reminds me of Nancy. She was a 24-year-old, learning-disabled young woman whose parents threw her out when they discovered she was pregnant.

At first Nancy was very suspicious of the shelter, its staff, volunteers and other guests. Nancy had been treated so poorly by adults that she reacted negatively to all vestiges of authority.

Very slowly she began to fit into the family. She relaxed when we told her that she could stay with us for the last four months of her pregnancy. We assured her of our love and reminded her we weren't letting her go! At this reassurance, she melted and let us into her highly-barricaded world.

Eight a.m. is wake-up time for guests in our house, so each morning I'd tap on her door and sing, "Rise and shine, show God your glory."

She would call through the closed door, "Oh no, go away." But she came to love being serenaded, even at that ungodly hour of the day.

One day after Nancy had gone, I received a picture of the baby and a card containing these words:

To Mike Moran,

> I am very glad I met you at the INN, when I was there. It was like a second home to me. I miss you very much and your laugh and when you woke me up in the morning. I will keep in touch about my daughter and me. Please pray for us and I will too. You are a special person.

No, Nancy, *you* are the special person—undefeated and beautiful.

Street People

    As we continued to open new emergency and transitional shelters, it shocked us to realize that we were not serving the needs of the people who literally had no place to lay their heads, the street people. Our shelters are filled each night with abused women and their children, runaway and throwaway teenagers, and those evicted from their homes. Because of the fragility of their lives and their present homelessness, we don't want to complicate things by including seriously troubled people—those with psychological, emotional or substance abuse problems. At the same time, The INN knew it had to respond to such people who were showing up with more and more frequency and in overwhelming numbers at our soup kitchens. We needed a shelter for street people.

    We didn't know what model we wanted to use, but we did know the one to reject. We didn't want the armory scene of New York and other large cities throughout the country. There, 100 to 500 cots are set up barracks style for homeless street people. The mayhem that results, sometimes tragic, is unavoidable. Take, for example, the story of a shelter which had a shower where the water was controlled from the staff office. The homeless person would enter the shower and a staff member would turn on the water. One evening a man went into the shower and only scalding hot water came out of the tap. The door of the shower was jammed, and he couldn't get out. No one heard his cries for help because of the din of 200 men in one big room. He was scalded to death. The story, by the way, appeared in the *New York Times*, in a small article at the bottom of page 53. Imagine if that incident occurred at the Tennis Club to one of the members. It wouldn't have been buried on the back page. But our homeless are powerless, voiceless, and as invisible as our blindness dictates.

    The model we adopted for this shelter was that of the Partnership for the Homeless in New York City. They coordinate 135 churches and synagogues, each of which provides beds for six to ten homeless persons. The program is run by dedicated volunteers in each of the congregations.

    Our shelter for street people, the Mary Brennan INN

Night Shelter, opened in February 1988 for the winter months. We now open from October through April. We accept eight street men each night and recruit members of local churches and synagogues as volunteers.

I'll never forget the first night we opened. A guest arrived and as he walked in said, "This is like the Holiday Inn."

In realty it was eight cots set up in our soup kitchen in Hempstead, with the tables and chairs pushed to one side. This makeshift, terribly simple setting never deserved such praise. We do so little for our homeless that even such a paltry environment elicits glowing accolades.

The clean but makeshift area is enhanced by the presence of truly caring volunteers. They will sit for hours and listen to the tales of men whose tragic lives of poverty, abandonment and addiction leave little to the imagination. Who else will take the time and interest to listen to these stories of "salty saints." Isn't it ironic that these societal rejects will receive higher places in heaven than you or me. They are the ones Yahweh raves about and with whom Jesus gladly associated.

Within this group of street people we sometimes see new life and restored hope. When NEWS 12 produced a series on the homeless, they did an on-camera interview with Julio. He had been living in an abandoned building in Hempstead, eating out of garbage cans and talking to himself because no one else would listen. But one viewer listened and called me. "I want to offer a job and a temporary room to Julio, until he can get on his own." Julio went to work and now has a studio apartment in Freeport. He came back the other day, a year after his last meal at the soup kitchen, to make believers out of us, to prove he had truly been reborn.

The following winter we opened our second overnight shelter for eight street men in the former Our Lady of Loretto convent.

"I never thought I'd be sleeping in a convent!" was the reaction of our first guests.

This shelter remains open all year, thanks to the generosity of many volunteers. Sometimes, volunteers ask incredulously, "You expect me to sleep in the same place as eight street men?" But after a few experiences at the shelter, they realize the humanness of the situation. The men are tired from a long day on the street. They eat heartily and get to bed early, thankful for a shower and a warm place to sleep.

When the volunteers listen to the life stories of the guests, their response is, "Oh, God, that could be me."

We are all one step away from homelessness. It's an epidemic which affects all classes, races and religions. Our volunteers are humbled when they look into the eyes of the street people and see themselves reflected. Sometimes they'll say, "There but for God's grace go I." I scowl when I hear that. It implies that I've been saved because God gave me grace, but not that homeless person. I think God's love is universal; it knows no bounds. Sometimes it's just that I've gotten better breaks in life. Or maybe my upbringing, class and race contributed to my present condition.

God, your help is there for all of us. Teach us to open our minds and hearts to all people—no matter how different from us they are. May the homeless forgive us for not seeing ourselves in their eyes or seeing God in them.

Chapter 4

Giving
And Receiving

When was the last time you threw a party for 1,100 people? Well The INN did just that in September 1989—for its volunteers.

From time to time we have had small gatherings of volunteers to thank them for their work. We even had a fifth anniversary party for about 300 volunteers, complete with a "volunteer" fourteen piece dance band! But we had never been able to invite all 1,100 volunteers to a party.

In the Spring of 1989 a woman by the name of Joy Carter-Froehlich called and said she was anxious to do something special for The INN. She was not a volunteer, but wanted to help us honor our volunteers by hosting a party. She almost passed out when she heard how many volunteers we had, but this was a challenge to her. "I have a large home in Garden City with lots of property. I can have a tent erected and we'll have space for as many guests as arrive!"

It was as simple as that. She canvassed for money and donations of food and before we knew it 1,100 invitations had been mailed. The party was a huge success, with everyone feeling very much a part of The INN.

Without our huge host of volunteers, The INN could not exist. It's that simple! They cook and serve, clean, talk to our guests, do repairs and maintenance work and rehabilitate old houses. The professionals lend their expertise: doctors, lawyers, chiropractors, art therapists, social workers, builders, etc. We have been blessed by giftedness shared.

Yet, the most frequent statement I hear from the lips

of volunteers is: "These people do more for me than I could ever do for them."

The meeting of rich and poor, black and white, old and young, Catholic and Jew at The INN have done as much to bring peace on earth as the United Nations! When I sit down at a table and treat another person as an equal, then we have a mutual basis for understanding and respect.

The one quality we ask of our volunteers is that they treat our guests as they treat themselves—or even better! The other important quality is a good sense of humor, without which we would despair at the way people are forced to live.

Our volunteers range in age from Girl Scouts who bake brownies for our shelters, to octogenarians who knit afghans. We have children who collect toiletries and money and who send us notes like this one:

We sold popcorn and brownies
to get money for you.
From, Elyse

Retired people like Marty Monahan from the New York Telephone Pioneers Club, will call and say, "What do you need? Name it."

Once I said to no one in particular, "We need a new freezer." A week later a brand new freezer appeared at our door.

We have mentally retarded kids writing to show they care:

I brout things for you
toys and money. Love, Lauren

Students in the Adelphi School of Social Work do their internship with us. We attract the very wealthy, like the man who called and said that he and his wife would buy a condo which we could use for one of our homeless families, to the very poor, like the envelope we receive in the mail every few months with no name or return address—just one dollar bill inside. This always reminds me of the scripture story of the Widow's Mite, which illustrates God's pleasure when a widow gives of her need over a wealthy person who gives of his or her excess. Both are badly needed and well appreciated.

Volunteers donate everything—from the man who gave us his life supply of ties, to the woman who donated two cemetery plots. (Don't laugh, the former will help a homeless person get a job, and the latter will allow him or her a place to be buried.)

We can never thank that volunteer enough who makes her ocean-front house available for our staff and community for workshops and retreats. Knowing that we have a peaceful spot where we can send a burnt-out staff person to be renewed and reinvigorated is a great blessing. And thank God for the volunteer who donated $60,000 worth of stock with the remarks: "I'd rather you get it than Uncle Sam. With you I know it will go to the homeless and not get lost in bureaucracy."

Volunteers' Hearts Are Changed

I truly believe that working at The INN is co-creating with God. We help to provide new options in life for our guests, and we re-create our own heart—changing hearts of stone into hearts of flesh. We are also creating the reign of God here on earth. The INN is a preview of what we can expect in the next life. All the classifications which divide us, race, religion, sex and age will be wiped away and we will be as one.

At The INN, you constantly get a sense of this "oneness." Carol, a live-in community member, has often said, "I have changed so much since I am here. My friends don't recognize me anymore because of my attitudes and opinions. I used to be so closed-minded. I was raised in an Italian-Catholic home and I thought that represented the whole world. Now I meet many different, unusual people. I've met atheists, gays, former inmates, the mentally and emotionally disabled and I've discovered they're all people. Our lives intertwine and we learn from each other."

The fact that we are more alike than different manifests itself daily at The INN. Many volunteers tell me how often they are mistaken as guests. What a gift— that we might treat each other as equals just like God does. Indeed, God's grace is given equally to all. Perhaps it was upbringing, or background or family prestige, or educational opportunities, or just plain luck which has given me an "advantage" over others. It wasn't because God decided to love me more than that homeless person.

We're all loved equally, and it's up to those with better economic and social advantages to share with others.

So many virtues are learned from our guests. We help one another attain holiness through wholeness. The important thing is to enter into relationships with open minds, leaving all the prejudices and stereotypes behind.

Listen to some of the stories of our volunteers and the great impact The INN has had on their lives.

Bob

Bob was one of the many people sent by the Courts to volunteer with us. These community service workers have been found guilty of minor crimes as first time offenders.

Bob was extremely handy and was assigned to do maintenance work in one of our shelters. He would whistle while he worked and although it appeared that he was totally absorbed in his work, he kept a keen eye on the comings and goings of the guests. After about one month of working two days a week, the coordinator noticed that during his break Bob would sit on the floor and play with the children. Here was this strong, burly white man with little black kids sitting on his lap and calling him "grandpa" and he loved every minute of it. "They're just like my own grandchildren," he would say.

Joanne

Joanne is a community member in one of our shelters. One night when she was still a volunteer, one guest pulled a knife on another. She acted quickly and calmly, but persuasively. She managed to get things cooled off and get the knife. For the average person, this would have been the end. For Joanne it was an occasion of conversion and commitment. She said, "God was with me. I couldn't have done it alone. I think God is trying to tell me that this is where I belong. I've decided to move into the community!"

Louise

Louise is another incredible live-in community member. She has a full-time job as a private duty nurse, caring for a homebound boy with leukemia. His parents were so moved by her stories about the shelter that they wanted to do something. Here were two people with a dying son who could see beyond their own pain to the needs of others. Louise blurted out that we were always accepting food donations at the shelter. That very day the couple arranged for their milkman to deliver two dozen eggs and four quarts of milk once a week. Their son has since died, but the milk and eggs keep coming!

Lena

Lena was a 20-year-old community service worker who was found guilty of driving while intoxicated. Tragically, her drinking led to a serious car accident in which a young passenger in her car was killed. She was assigned to do household chores in one of our shelters.

Having come from a very wealthy family, Lena was not used to menial tasks around the house. Instead of resisting and doing the work grudgingly, she pitched right in and got her hands dirty. She worked, cleaned, smiled, scrubbed, laughed, and prepared fancy snacks for the guests. She became a favorite around the house. Guests would gather around and listen to her stories. Whenever she had the opportunity to speak with one of our guests who was a substance abuser, she would tell her own story of addiction and the tragedy that ensued. "I killed that boy," she'd tell her listeners, "Alcohol and drugs kill, you know."

Patti

Patti was taking a psychology course in college. It required a summer internship in a social service agency. She chose one or our shelters as her place of work.

She worked hard that summer, talking with the guests, listening to their stories of crisis, assisting them with the unending forms and documentation needed to establish themselves as public assistance recipients.

Sometimes she'd spend the whole day waiting with a guest at Social Services. Case workers have an average of about 250 clients, so a full day of waiting is routine.

One day she took Ken to the Department to wait with him, give him courage, and try to be his advocate. After weeks of helping him to assemble the needed documentation, Ken was approved as a public assistance recipient. The next day he stepped off the sidewalk into the direct path of a speeding car and was killed instantly.

This experience caused Patti many introspective moments. "What's life all about? What am I doing here? Why are some people's lives so filled with pain and tragedy?"

At the conclusion of eight weeks work, she said, "I was raised a Catholic but somewhere along the line I lost my faith. But I found it again here in this house. I truly believe that God has placed me here. I find God all over this house. I have a new awareness about God's action in my life and in the lives of others. I was planning to go into business and make lots of money. But now I've got to re-evaluate the direction of my life. Maybe I need to become a social worker. These people—guests, staff and volunteers—have had a deep impact on my life."

Vicki

Vicki was an 18-year-old community service worker who needed to give 20 hours of service. The shelter coordinator introduced her to the guests as a "volunteer" rather than exposing her as someone who had committed a crime.

Vicki worked hard and got to know some of the guests well. At the end of her service, with tears in her eyes, she spoke to the shelter coordinator. "Thanks for initially introducing me as a volunteer rather than a community service worker. I wish I had come on my own rather than having been forced to be here. I've been so touched by the people I've met—guests, volunteers, community members. I wish I had known about their special world before.

Maryellen

Maryellen is a news writer for a major New York City radio station. She lives on Long Island and heard about The INN through her church.

She started volunteering on weekends at one of our shelters. One Saturday she arrived to find Ruby, a forty-year-old black woman who had been released from the hospital to our shelter. The hospital released her without checking to see if she was adequately dressed. With bare feet, she arrived at our door.

Maryellen was horrified. She drove Ruby to the thrift shop located above our soup kitchen in Hempstead. They not only found shoes, but a complete outfit to go with them. The whole ensemble actually matched. Ruby was so thrilled at being "bedecked like a princess" (as she put it), that she ran downstairs and in view of the 200 guests at the soup kitchen, our "princess" danced and sang for joy. Maryellen, in reflecting on this and similar experiences at the shelter, commented: "Never have I met people so ecstatic over simple things in life."

Joan

Joan volunteered at our Hicksville INN on Mondays and commuted to her job in the city during the rest of the week.

One day she realized that a man she served at The INN was the same man she bought a newspaper from every day at the Hicksville train station. "He was always so friendly and kind, whether I was serving him or he was serving me."

Rubin was his name, and he was well-known in the neighborhood as "the homeless man who pushed his cart filled with all his possessions." One rainy night as he maneuvered his cart along the side of the road, a car careened into him, killing him instantly.

The local community was so upset over the tragic end of this kind-hearted man, that they quickly gathered forces and, with Joan in the lead, planned a special farewell to Rubin. The neighborhood funeral home donated the funeral services, someone offered a cemetery plot, and the local churches planned an interfaith memorial service.

Three hundred people gathered to bid farewell to a man who through his death brought people of different faiths together to ponder the needs of the homeless.

Adrian

Adrian was the director of a social service agency in Nassau County. He was interested in the plight of the homeless and volunteered to assist us in obtaining some grant money to be used in our work.

One day he stopped at the soup kitchen and without letting anyone know his identity, he stood on line for a meal. "I was treated with such respect and dignity, both by the volunteers and the other guests and I was so moved by all that I saw, that I went home and wrote this poem."

IS THERE STILL TIME?

From nowhere they appear as noon
    hour draws close once more
And suddenly there's a line where a
    bare wall stood before.
A gray-bearded man with years of
    work etched firmly on his face
Is followed by an elderly lady who
    waits her turn in place.
A man without a coat, a fellow
    without a shoe,
A lady with a baby, and a pair of
    teenagers too,
A very thin man with dark, dark
    rings under his baggy eyes
Appears upset and looks about when
    he hears the baby cry.
A young couple come up the block
    and take their place in line
As countless others join the scene
    and line up right behind.
No gold chains, no Cabbage Patch dolls,
    no fancy clothes are seen,
For in the cold, cold world of poverty,
    there are no designer jeans,

But tattered clothes take their place
    and a coat no matter how old
Is often treasured beyond belief
    and worth far more than gold.
What is it that draws these folks
    to join this vulnerable crew
Some bread, some soup, perhaps some stew,
    a kind word, or maybe two...

Rose Marie

Rose Marie came to volunteer in one of our shelters and was appalled at the shabby way the homeless are treated by case workers. She has had more than one good battle with a case manager at the Department of Social Services, reminding them that they're supposed to be making life more livable for their homeless clients, not more unbearable.

Rose Marie knew that she needed more than a good heart and a big mouth to assist in changing an unjust social system. So, in her late fifties she went back to school for her Masters in Social Work. "I never thought I'd go back to school, but I saw a need and just knew I had to do something about it." She graduated with honors, and is now employed by The INN to work directly with our guests. We know a good deal when we see it!

Sue

Sue is a teacher in Far Rockaway. She volunteered as a cook for three years in one of our shelters. She became increasingly upset by the number of children who weren't in school, or who missed a great deal of school due to their homelessness. Until recently, the school system discriminated against homeless school-aged children. The neighborhood school where the homeless child came from said, "We don't want her, she's not living in our school district since she moved to the shelter." The school where the shelter is located said, "That's not her permanent home, so we have no obligation to take her." Finally the Supreme Court ruled that the parent or guardian could choose between the two schools. It took legislation to provide the right to education for our homeless kids!

Sue decided that she could apply some of her teaching expertise to assist homeless children. She began an after-school program for "shelter kids" who were behind in their studies.

Cathy

Cathy's husband has a good job and her children are in school. She got tired of cleaning her house and attending endless coffee klatches where "my neighbors" business is the order of the day."

She volunteered to work at our main office and is now involved in "organizing her neighbors' business" by coordinating volunteers for our soup kitchens and shelters. She's always coming up with new ideas like having a conference day for people who work with the homeless.

Marty

Marty was volunteering at one of our shelters for about three years. He's a quiet, kind, gentle man who could listen intently to the problems and concerns of our guests. Then personal tragedy struck him. His second marriage was ending in disaster. His wife had walked out, taking with her many of his treasured possessions, and threatening to get his last penny.

Through months of anxiety and distress, he never missed a Thursday night at the shelter. "I need to come to volunteer. There are so many truly good people here that it restores my faith in humankind."

Carol

Carol was a Garden City socialite. She attended as many cocktail parties and bought as many dresses as she could. Finally she got fed up with what she called the "shallowness of evaluating myself on my wealth and popularity."

The first day she arrived to volunteer at the soup kitchen she was dressed in high fashion clothes and wore lots of jewelry so "they'd know I wasn't one of them." Conversion happens slowly and deeply. Six months later she was arriving in jeans and no makeup, "So they'll think I'm one of them."

She now serves as coordinator of volunteers one day a week at the soup kitchen, assists every Thursday at a shelter, and brings in clothing for our guests. She has visited some of our folks in prison and arranged to place more than one young man in a detox or residential rehabilitation program. The best thing about Carol is she's learned how to look directly into the eyes of our guests and see the beauty and strength there.

Jim

One day Jim called me at my office. "I'm a retired man, but I'm real good with my hands. I called Fr. Bruce Ritter and asked if I could volunteer at Covenant House. They told me they didn't need me. So, if you want me, you can have me."

"Come right over," I replied.

That was the beginning of Jim's volunteer career with The INN. To say he is good with his hands is an understatement. This talented handyman has rehabilitated one soup kitchen and four shelters. He is always available in case something breaks down and needs immediate attention. He has a garage full of parts—no matter what material is needed for a repair, Jim always has it.

One day we were laying rugs in a recently rehabilitated shelter. "I don't know," said Jim, "you're sure no Mother Teresa. She throws out the rugs because it's more like penance to have a bare floor. And here we are, putting down carpeting."

"Well," I replied "that's where Mother Teresa and I disagree. I believe the poor need beauty and a homelike atmosphere as much as we do—perhaps even more. If you hear Mother Teresa is throwing out more carpeting, let's go pick it up!"

Jim just shrugged his shoulders, completely bewildered at my seemingly sacrilegious comments!

Carol Ann

Carol Ann is a community member in one of our shelters. She often recalls how she learned more about herself through our guest, John.

John had just been released from prison and his

family had disowned him. He had no place to go, and was referred to our shelter by the prison chaplain.

John was enterprising and had soon landed a job as a restaurant chef. He came alive and fell into the routine of the house, sometimes cooking at the shelter too. He was one of the most gentle and helpful guests we had ever known.

One day after he had been with us about three weeks, Carol Ann was helping him fill out a report for his parole officer. She learned that he'd been in prison twice, both times for being an accessory to a murder!

"I almost passed out when I realized that sitting with me was an accused murderer. Yet he was one of the most gentle and helpful people I'd met. If I had known his record before he came, I'm sure I would never have accepted him into our house. Yet once I knew him, I believed his story, and count him as one of our successes."

After John got an apartment of his own, he'd come back to visit and often expressed his gratitude to Carol Ann for believing in him.

Carol Ann has since said, "I learned from John not to prejudge people so I never read the past history of new guests. I want to accept and come to know them as they present themselves to me, not based on some ancient history. After all, if they knew my past, perhaps they'd reject me! We give one another respect. I am what I am here and now. Give me a chance to prove myself—to keep what's good and change what needs to go."

Aurelie

Aurelie lived for five years as a community member worker in one of our shelters. When she left she was sixty-seven years old. She's our own Mother Teresa, without the Nobel Peace Prize.

She believed that in our shelters, "The Gospel is not preached—it's lived. Living here has made me appreciate my vocation to religious life. Living in a convent you take everything for granted. You depend on the Sisters to do everything. Sometimes without realizing it you fall into living a middle-class existence. I could do that as a lay person. Here you meet and live with poor people and learn what life is all about. I love our prayer life too, not just formalized ritual and prayers out of a book. We each take turns leading prayer and the creativity is amazing. Everyday is a festival and filled with little miracles. Last Thanksgiving Day we had a meal fit for a king and queen but we had forgotten dessert. There were no fattening goodies to end the sumptuous turkey dinner. Suddenly the doorbell rang and to our surprise, a neighbor stood there with three freshly baked glorious pies. 'There really is a God,' I cried out!"

Dolores

Dolores is a retired school teacher who lives in Garden City. She got bored lounging around the house, watching her housekeeper clean. She arrived to volunteer at one of our shelters with the word, "I don't do windows."

Five years of volunteering behind her, she continues to come weekly to our shelter. What does she do? "What else—I clean the shelter, and you know something, I even do the windows!"

Joyce

Joyce is a live-in community member. She was discouraged at seeing so much pain in the lives of our guests. The following event converted her, calmed her and caused her to renew her commitment to living at the shelter. Here's her story.

"An eight-year-old boy was here with his alcoholic mother. She paid little if any attention to him. Moving from shelter to shelter, she had neglected his schooling. He had hardly ever been to school, and didn't even know the alphabet or how to write his name. I worked with him evenings, teaching him to read and write. One night he threw his arms around me and asked, 'Can I stay here and live with you all the time and you can be my mother?' "

These are only some of the countless stories of conversion at The INN.

Chapter 5

Twelve Gifts

Working and living with the homeless has caused me to live life more fully. At first I thought I was wonderful for devoting my life to the homeless. Now I realize that I am what I am today because of what I've learned from them. Homeless people have given me far more than I could ever offer them.

There are twelve virtues or gifts homeless people have given to me. They are precious lessons in life for which I pause, meditate upon, and offer praise to God. These are the virtues I have learned from the homeless— not from their mouths but from the example of their lives.

Trust In God

The homeless have taught me that even though times are difficult, I must trust in God and renew my belief in the ability of prayer to transform myself and the world. Mary was an especially good teacher in this regard.

Mary has three children. She stayed with us for one month until she was placed by the Department of Social Services in a horrible apartment with leaks and bugs and little heat. She went to Nassau/Suffolk Law Services and they fought for her cause until she was placed in a decent apartment.

One day she brought a woman and her two children to a shelter. Mary assured her it was nice and safe and came with her for reassurance. The person on duty asked Mary how she managed to survive the difficult times she had endured. She replied: "I just kept praying to the Lord all the time, and I never gave up hope because I knew it was in the Lord's hands, and that God would watch over me and give us what we needed. It wasn't what I wanted, but what God wanted, and I knew it would all work our somehow."

Patience

Mary had to have patience, but Sandy taught me even more about this virtue of living day to day, one moment at a time, sitting for what seemed endless days in the waiting room of the Department of Social Services, ready to scream but instead quietly attentive.

Sandy left an abusive husband after years of an impossible marriage. She had a son, Michael, who was a terror. He was hyperactive and needed constant attention. They lived with us for a little over a month and finally were placed in a tiny studio apartment in Freeport. Sandy patiently cared for her son and his needs and continued to fight for a divorce from her abusive husband. About a year later, the divorce was finalized and her ex-husband moved out of their house by court order. She was finally able to return to her own home. Her long-standing patience had won the day.

Not being one to rest on her laurels, she immediately thought about others whose patience was wearing thin. She called us one day happy and excited because now that she had her own home again she could help others who had been in her situation. "Is there anyone there who needs a place to stay? They can come and live with us." It was just another way of saying thank you.

Perseverance

The ability to put up a good fight and not give up until a resolution is reached was taught me by Eugenia. She had been evicted because she couldn't meet her rent payments due to the meager amount of money given to her as a welfare recipient.

She came to one of our shelters with her three children. After being with us about five weeks, still unable to locate an affordable apartment (landlords don't want to rent to people on welfare, especially if they have children) she was placed for three months in a run-down welfare motel. She kept fighting with the Department of

Social Services to help her find a decent apartment, and finally she was placed in Hempstead.

At the Valentine's Day "Have a Heart for the Homeless Vigil" she spoke to 1,000 people about her own long struggle and encouraged others not to give up. She is intelligent, attractive, well-spoken and wants to give talks around Long Island so that, as she says, "people might realize the problem is a real one, that the homeless don't deserve the treatment they get, and that something must be done so others don't have to go through what my family did."

Generosity

I learned about generosity from Bob. Although the homeless are in crisis and pain, they reach out to help others in need.

Bob had a wonderful job with a major New York newspaper. He was arrested for tax evasion. During his year in prison, his wife wiped him out financially, sold the house and car and took off. When he was released from prison he had nowhere to go, and he came to live at our shelter.

Because of his skills, he was rehired by the same newspaper and within one month had enough money to live on his own.

Now he's a volunteer. He comes back on the average of twice a month to cook, but most of all to lend an ear to our guests who need to talk. Recently he said: "I like coming here and I always enjoy talking to the guests. I learn a lot about human nature, and I learn to deal with my own problems better and not be so self-centered. Other people are a lot worse off and whatever I can do to ease their burden I want to do."

Humility/Simplicity

Our homeless guests teach me how to be humble and to develop child-like simplicity. Pam is a good example for me. She left an abusive live-in boyfriend and came to live in one of our shelters. She assisted with household chores, and managed to get three part-time jobs so she could save up enough money to get her own place. She finally set up her own studio and was so excited that her spirit was contagious. Many volunteers gave her house-warming gifts to help her get started. The night she left, she said tearfully: "I feel like I'm a child leaving home for the first time in my life."

Survival

Our guests have been through hard times and have learned to survive. Sometimes they have had to be street-wise and watch out for themselves so others wouldn't take advantage of them. They've given me lessons in how to be tough when that's what's needed.

Billy is a good example of this virtue. At seventeen, he was an impulsive, angry, abusive teenager. He came from a broken home. He turned to dealing drugs and was arrested.

After his release from prison, he came to stay with us since his family would have nothing to do with him. He exhibited all the signs of a self-possessed, macho man. He loved women and believed that they all loved him! He was given a pair of new white jeans, which he promptly took and redesigned—by slashing holes in them, particularly the seat. This way he was truly keeping up with fashion!

We gave him a lot of love and he began to mellow and to trust us. He even volunteered to speak at a high school about what it's really like to get mixed up with drugs.

For all of his macho veneer, and his "street wisdom" which he needed to survive, he was still a child, and spent an entire evening in tears telling a volunteer how his mother wouldn't have anything to do with him and the thing he most desired was to earn her love.

Acceptance

It's amazing what tolerance and understanding our guests have for each other. They live and let live and don't allow lifestyle to be a barrier to relationships.

Randy was a transvestite who stayed in our shelter for one week. When he arrived, we weren't sure of the sex of this new guest. We were particularly concerned about the reaction of the other guests and how Randy would be treated.

It turned out that the live-in community had more of a problem than our guests who treated Randy like one of the family. And you know something Randy treated those of us who had prejudged him/her with kindness and understanding.

Appreciation

It always surprises me that despite the awkwardness and embarrassment many of our guests feel at being in a shelter, they always find it in them to say thank you. Take, for example, Marion.

Marion was a forty-three year old woman with two boys. She had been burned out of her apartment in Long Beach by developers who wanted to "gentrify the neighborhood."

We celebrated her birthday while she was with us, offering a cake and a few small gifts. She thanked us profusely and said she was deeply touched because "this is the first time in my life that anyone has ever had a birthday cake for *my* birthday."

Remembering

Homeless people seem never to forget their past, even after they leave us. They remember where they've been, and reach out to help others who are where they were.

Pat called me in my office one day and said, "Three years ago my husband abused me and my three kids. He threw us out of the house and we had nowhere to go. The St. Vincent de Paul Society gave me some money and helped pay the first two months' rent in a nice apartment. I was shocked at this unexpected generosity, and said 'But how will I repay you?' They replied, 'Pat, when you get on your feet help someone else who's in need.' Well, I'm on my feet, I have a job and the kids are in school. I'd like to help, but I want to give more than money. I want to offer service." Now every Thursday at noon you can find Pat in our Hicksville soup kitchen serving coffee to the people who eat there. "How could I forget my roots?" she comments simply.

Life-Giving

Homeless people are each other's best therapists. They know when to listen, when to give advice, and when to just be present to one another. They've taught me lessons in how to be life-giving to others.

Kim was an abused woman who arrived at our shelter late one night. She was unable to sleep and sat in the living room. Another guest Anne, heard her wandering about and came out of her room. Anne sat and listened until 2 a.m. as Kim described in detail the terrible trial she'd been through. Anne cried softly and then opened up, telling her own story of abuse. They stayed up all night comforting one another.

The next day one of the community members, who heard what had happened during the night, thanked Anne for being so caring. She replied, "I've been there myself. I never would have made it if people hadn't helped me. I think I owe it to them to help her. But, you know, it helped me too. I realized I've come a long way and I'm not alone. I was feeling sorry for myself but now I see there are people who are hurting more than me. It's not right to be so totally self-absorbed anymore."

Sense Of Humor

In the midst of their problems and anguish, our guests never lose their sense of humor. They've made me laugh and forget about my own problems, which at times are miniscule compared to theirs.

One good example for me was Gail. She was an older woman whose adult children had rejected her and refused to let her live with them. Yet, Gail still knew how to laugh. She kept us all howling with her funny jokes and stories from when she was a child star on Broadway. She always said, "Things are so hard, but who wants to sit up in their room crying alone, it's better to be down here laughing with other people."

Celebration

Finally, our guests have the gift of being able to really celebrate. Their ability to rejoice in life, even when times are tough, has been a special blessing in our shelter.

I'm reminded of Shelton and Josette. They were an interracial couple with an 18-month-old daughter. They were both 19 years old and had been living with his parents who disapproved of his desire to marry a white girl. They kicked out the couple and their newly born baby.

They came to stay with us and after one week, they went to City Hall to get married. That night we had a special dinner for them, complete with a toast (grape juice, of course) and a wedding cake. Josette cried and said "I never thought I'd have a wedding reception. And you know something, this is the best one I've ever attended!"

I've learned so many good things from our guests. Their virtues have enriched my life.

Chapter 6

The Future of The INN:

Challenging The Institutions

Where does The INN go from here? I would summarize our future goals as these:

1. To continue to respond to the needs of local communities in addressing the hunger and homeless problems there. This will entail opening new soup kitchens and shelters.
2. To advocate for the rights of the homeless, especially for permanent, low-cost housing.
3. To continue to raise the consciousness of the general public and our elected officials, and to demand legislative and systemic change to address homelessness.
4. To open and manage permanent housing units for poor people on Long Island. These include single-family homes as well as multiple-dwelling apartments and SRO's (single room occupancy facilities).
5. To increase staff and volunteers to adequately address the growing number of homeless on Long Island.

THE FUTURE OF THE INN CONSISTS IN PUTTING ITSELF OUT OF BUSINESS. As proud as we are of our accomplishments, we sincerely regret the reason for them. The only way we can put ourselves out of business is to attack the systemic issues causing poverty and perpetuating a permanent underclass. We must challenge the institutions which feed these problems. Those are not easy issues to address.

Sometimes I see our present efforts as a bandaid approach, running around feeding and sheltering, when the deeper wounds keep festering and the malignancy continues to spread. I believe that the deepest wound is a social system gone sour and critically in need of change. Emergency food and shelter are essential but they are only the beginning. Our volunteers have taken the first steps by dishing out soup and making the beds. But when we suggest that it's time to challenge the county executive or, far worse, agitate for housing for low-income people in their neighborhood—too often they turn and walk away. We must move our volunteers from a stance of charity to one of justice. We must convince them that the way to attack the problem of homelessness is to challenge the very institutions which make up our society. These institutions include government, religion and the "isms": racism, classism, ageism and sexism.

Challenging the Government

Today there are 3 million homeless people in the United States. At the present rate of increase, there will be 19 million homeless people in our country by the year 2000.

These shocking statistics cause us to blush with anger when we realize that during the Reagan years military expenses continually increased as the budget for human services decreased. During that era, we experienced a 75 percent cut in monies set aside for housing for low-income people while our budget for bombs increased dramatically.

In answer to government's inhuman priorities, a vision statement was circulated by the organizers of the "Housing Now" rally at the 1989 *March on Washington for the Homeless*. "We commit ourselves...to call for changes in national priorities which would shift funding from military spending to programs which enhance the quality of life for all people. These programs would be directed toward providing housing for all persons, full employment at adequate wages, access to health care, child care, and educational opportunities for all."

The issue of housing is particularly difficult when you consider the severe lack of decent and affordable housing on Long Island. Making matters worse is the scandalous news of fraud by officials, i.e., Department of Housing and Urban Development (HUD) and locally elected officials. It's impossible to identify the real criminal when government officials divert properties from the so-called "welfare cheats."

Overcrowded living conditions among the poor are typical in Nassau and Suffolk. We know landlords who will lay down ten cots in their living room and rent them to ten singles! Some landlords have discovered an even better money-making scheme. They rent out rooms on an 8-hour basis. Within 24 hours three tenants or families come to sleep in three consecutive 8-hour shifts. The greatest travesty of justice is that the Department of Social Services pays rent to some of these landlords for the public assistance clients placed there!

Why not close down these illegal apartments? The fact is that at least 50 percent of the rental apartments on Long Island are illegal. Vacancies are almost non-existent. If we tried to regulate illegal housing, it would primarily result in evicting working class and poor people, adding to the homeless problem.

Many of us who work with the homeless are outraged by the lack of housing, not only on Long Island but across our nation. On October 7, 1989 a "Housing Now" coalition of people called for a *March on Washington for the Homeless*. The purpose was to draw media attention to the problem and evoke a response from our elected officials. Basically we were demanding a reinstatement of those housing funds cut during the Reagan years.

The march was a huge success. *The Washington Post* reported 40,000 participants, *Newsday* said there were 150,000 and the *New York Times* said it was somewhere in between! Those of us who attended, including about forty of the INN's homeless guests, know that we were at least 100,000 strong.

"Since you did not attend the rally, President Bush and HUD Secretary, Jack Kemp, were you at least

- 93 -

watching? How can you turn a deaf ear to the cries of the poor?"

A marcher's banner posted on the bolted front doors of the Department of Justice read: "We want shelter from the rain, not tax-shelters."

To all our elected officials: "We put you there to represent not only the wealthy, but the poor as well (or perhaps, especially). Poor people often don't vote for you, or for anyone, because too often they have no residence and are busy keeping themselves alive. They are in desperate need of your help. Don't turn away!"

What can The INN do to respond to this critical need for long-term, low-cost housing? Realizing we could accomplish very little alone, we assisted in organizing the Nassau Suffolk Coalition for the Homeless. This group is two years old and consists of 250 members—half are agencies, organizations, churches and synagogues. The other half of the members are interested individuals. Together we advocate for the rights of the homeless on Long Island. We have centered much of our attention around housing issues for the homeless—emergency, transitional and permanent, low-cost housing.

On Valentines Day, 1989 we organized a *Have a Heart for the Homeless Candlelight Vigil* at the United Way in Melville. Over 1,000 people demanded more attention and more funding to address the needs of the homeless. They openly defied the "not in my backyard syndrome" by stating that we are all responsible for advocating for housing—even if it is in my backyard! We had excellent speakers, from homeless people to Suffolk County Executive Patrick Halpin.

The Coalition used this media event to advance one of its demands. Both the Nassau and Suffolk County Executives have been asked to donate 10 percent of county-owned properties to not-for-profit agencies so that boarded-up houses will be rehabilitated and vacant property built upon, as a means of increasing the housing stock for low-income people.

At present both counties auction-off their property, most of which has been repossessed by the County through mortgage-defaults. I've attended these yearly auctions and have observed that many of the bidders are speculators who buy the house and either board it up and wait for a change in the real estate market, or do minimal rehabilitation work and then rent a one-family house to three or four (or more) families. Other bidders at the auction turn out to be crack dealers. Since these auctions require a cash purchase, crack dealers are in a good position to qualify. They buy the house and use it as a base for their operations or a residence for their dealers.

The Coalition wants to reverse this. We are asking for 10 percent, a mere tithing, of the available properties. Our not-for-profit groups will receive the house, repair it with grant money now available from New York State, and place public assistance families in these residences. The rent allowance they receive each month from the Department of Social Services will be turned over to the not-for-profit agency and this will be supplemented by a federal subsidy through a Section 8 certificate. This will allow the groups to pay operating expenses plus maintain the house and property in good condition. The not-for-profit agency then agrees to be the owner and landlord, and also commits itself to provide a case manager to assist the family with the social service, medical, educational and personal needs of the family, and to trouble shoot and keep this family in permanent housing and out of shelters and welfare motels. In the long run, government money will be saved and people's lives will be changed.

Suffolk County has agreed to turn over some properties for this worthy purpose and Nassau County is studying our proposal.

Since "low-cost housing" is not a popular political cause, foot-dragging is not unusual. Properties which can be auctioned rather than given away could bring in additional revenues. Only if the coalition can rally enough voters and property owners to join in the chorus demanding affordable housing, will we see movement in Nassau county.

In the meantime, The INN has been informed by Suffolk County that it has approved our application for twenty surplus properties. The County will turn over five pieces initially, to test out our ability to build and manage the houses and provide social service support to the families.

This is a small but very significant step for The INN. We are now moving from a bandaid approach to attacking the root cause of the disease. By providing decent housing and support services, we hope to restore some dignity and self-worth to broken people.

The INN is also attempting to establish some decent housing opportunities for singles. We have had a severe problem in placing singles from our shelters in decent, permanent housing. There are few legal boarding houses left on Long Island, and no certificates are being issued for new ones. Most of the legal boarding houses have become crack and alcohol dens.

We have purchased a legal two-family house which has four bedrooms in each apartment. Residents are selected from among the guests who come to our shelters. We accept from each guest only the amount they receive each month for rent from the Department of Social Services. The house will be drug and alcohol free, and the residents will be required to follow guidelines which have been established for their own safety and privacy. An INN case manager will regularly visit the house and assist residents with their needs. Efforts will be made to help them to live together communally, sharing tasks and providing a dignified and congenial space for one another.

Finally, The INN is most conscious of its responsibility to provide long-term housing for that most vulnerable population of homeless people: persons with AIDS. We have recently re-opened our residence for people with AIDS. This time we are providing a comprehensive staff which will attend to the physical, social, emotional, therapeutic, spiritual and recreational needs of our guests. We will do our best to provide a loving setting which will allow these special people to prepare for death as they live life fully at The INN.

Local Authorities

If The INN has had its hands full understanding the federal government and its response to the homeless, we have had to wring our hands in despair at local authorities.

Mayors are not happy when a soup kitchen comes to town. First of all, it certainly does not look good that there are hungry people in their town or village. The general myth which must be upheld goes something like this: "Long Island is the American dream come true. Hunger and homelessness are rampant in the city, not here. Those of us who came to Long Island moved away from those city problems. If there are hungry people, they must have come out from the city to enjoy the good life. But don't feed them, or they'll stay."

This myth is indeed a misperception. The people we feed and house are long-term Nassau and Suffolk residents. The majority have lived here all their lives. It's the high cost of living on Long Island combined with the low-wage scale which has caused poor people to end up without sufficient food, clothing and housing. When you consider that two-thirds of the homeless on Long Island are women and children, we are talking of an exploding feminization of poverty.

Mayors on Long Island don't want to face this reality. It certainly does not look good for their administration if an increasing number of their constituents are hungry and homeless. Nor does the existence of a soup kitchen ingratiate the mayor with local merchants and residents.

I'll never forget the mayor's visit to the Hempstead soup kitchen. We had been open about three months and the mayor had received complaints from local merchants because of long lines of people outside the soup kitchen.

The mayor walked in one day unannounced. He brushed aside a plate of food that was offered to him and walked up to Pat O'Connor, "What do you think you're doing here in this church?" he demanded.

"Nothing less than a church should do. We're feeding hungry people." Pat replied.

The mayor curiously observed the crowd of 100 and turned to Pat and blurted out, "My God, I never realized there were so many hungry people in Hempstead."

I guess the shock of this scene kept him quiet for a while, but about six months later he exerted enough pressure upon our host church so that our one-year lease was not renewed. We went to another church the following year and then to a third church. Each time the mayor couldn't withstand the complaints of the local merchants, and so he successfully pressured the pastors to evict us.

The same phenomenon continues to play itself out in town after town on Long Island, where the local authorities can't work things out between the merchants and the soup kitchens. It is not politically fashionable on Long Island, as it is in New York City, to espouse the cause of the homeless.

There has been one notable exception. The mayor of Glen Cove called and asked me to speak with the local clergy about the need for a soup kitchen and/or shelter. Here was one brave mayor taking his head out of the sand and addressing a vital social issue on his locale. Instead of chasing The INN out of town as some mayors had done, he was inviting us in!

As it happened I did meet with the clergy who recognized the need, but were nervous about a group house for the mentally disabled which opened despite local opposition. Several articles in the local paper forewarned the residents that a soup kitchen was in the offing. Yet at the first planned meeting, 175 people arrived, not to protest the opening of a soup kitchen, but to volunteer their services. And eight months later the North Shore INN opened its doors!

Yet another happy miracle was born on Long Island's north shore. This area of Long Island is known as "The Gold Coast" since many of the rich and famous reside there. It's unthinkable to speak about hunger and homelessness in this exclusive area.

The "miracle" happened on a cold February night several years ago. I was at home and the phone rang, "Mike Moran, this is Tom DiNapoli, Assemblyman from Great Neck. I'm sorry to bother you at home, but I don't know what to do. My office is smack in the middle of the main street in beautiful Great Neck and would you believe, I just found a homeless woman sleeping in the stairwell of my office building. Mike, you have to do something about this." "No, Tom," I countered, "WE have to do something about this."

That woman received shelter, but the bigger issue remained: homelessness even in Great Neck.

Tom and I met several weeks later and he subsequently visited our soup kitchen in Hempstead. What delighted me so much was that he came without photographers (a politician's trademark), and spent the morning in the kitchen volunteering. Now, there's a politician after my own heart! If more of our elected officials stopped discussing the homeless problem and spent a morning volunteering at a soup kitchen or shelter, their responses would be genuine rather than dictated by political urgency.

Nassau and Suffolk Counties, too, have given The INN a share of grief. The Departments of Health routinely make recommendations to us based on restaurant procedure but our limited funds do not always allow us to bring our operation up to restaurant codes. Please don't misunderstand me, we keep our kitchens and dining rooms very clean, and we are extremely careful to handle food properly, but we are not operating a restaurant.

Recently Marge Archer, a founder of the Claddagh INN in Arverne, was summoned before the judge for certain violations of the restaurant code.

The judge said, "You must get a restaurant license."

Marge tried to explain that when you feed 100 hungry people in twenty minutes because they're waiting at the door, you can't always abide by every regulation codified for restaurants. The judge continued to reprimand her and finally Marge, in utter frustration, blurted out: "Does Mother Teresa have a restaurant license?" There was complete silence in the courtroom. The judge then lifted the gavel and proclaimed "This case is dismissed!"

Several years ago an East Meadow librarian called my office. "My library is becoming a day shelter."

"What do you mean?"

"There are more and more people hanging out here just to get out of the cold. They're homeless and they sit here all day. I don't have the heart to throw them out as long as they're quiet, but the numbers are growing. One day I called the Department of Social Services. 'I have a man and his wife who are sleeping in their car, can you help them?'

'Nonsense, there are no homeless people in Nassau County,' was the response.

I couldn't believe it! 'But I know they are. I've brought blankets to their car in the Waldbaum's parking lot. I know they're homeless. And I have a family at the library who don't have enough to eat. I bring extra sandwiches from home for them, can't you help them?'

'Nonsense!' she insisted. 'There are no hungry people in Nassau County.'

I persisted and argued with the worker until she finally admitted that it was *policy* to say that no one is hungry or homeless in Nassau County."

It's so disheartening! The very department which should give the most assistance to the homeless responds inadequately and sometimes inappropriately. The alleged *policy* of the Department of Social Services to deny the reality of suffering people, is an immoral policy. But policies come down from the top. We must find out who initiated this policy and what we can do to change it.

There are several other problem areas within the Department of Social Services in both counties. One is the proportion of workers to clients. The present ratio is 1 to 250. How can we expect one worker to deal effectively with so many needy and hurting people? That proportion is scandalous.

The Department also has some questionable procedures. The workers are trained to discourage individuals from seeking public assistance. The interview goes like this, "What do you mean you need government help? Don't you have family and friends who can house and feed you? Are you that unpopular that you can't turn to someone else for assistance?"

The Department also uses "Greyhound therapy" to rid itself of potential clients. "Your brother lives in Ohio. We'll pay for your transportation if you'll move there so he can take care of you." Sometimes the Department will *transfer* a case to a neighboring county by getting them housing there. "Now you can go to the Department of Social Service in that county when you need help. Don't come back to us!"

All of these unjust and inhumane practices must be rooted out and replaced by a more caring system.

This brings me, finally, to our County Executives. They must be convinced by us, the voters, that they were elected to care not only for constituents who have money, but for the poor and homeless who have no money and no political clout.

That is one of the reasons that the Nassau Suffolk Coalition for the homeless was founded in 1988. This group consists of about 125 social service agencies, organizations, churches and synagogues and an equal number of interested individual members. The task of the Coalition is to advocate for the rights of the homeless, particularly in terms of emergency, transitional and most importantly, permanent, affordable housing for the homeless.

There are glimmers of hope—like the *Have a Heart for the Homeless Candlelight Vigil.* Suffolk County Executive Patrick Halpin spoke to over 1,000 people that night about his concerns for the poor and what Suffolk is doing to address the problems of the homeless.

We have not had equal interest from Mr. Gulotta. Is it necessary for more people to freeze to death on the streets of Nassau for us to convince him that the problems are real and immediate? I sincerely hope not.

Public officials, we implore you to open your eyes and ears, but most importantly your hearts, to the cry of the poor. Tomorrow may be too late!

Challenging Religion

Should religious groups have anything to do with the hungry and homeless? I would say if a church does not reach out to those in need, it has no right being called church. Furthermore, if a church does not develop a special program to assist the poor, it is failing in its most important mission.

The obligation of addressing the needs of the most vulnerable is clearly specified in our Judeo-Christian scriptures. The following prayer service originally used at the Intercommunity Center for Justice and Peace is designed to highlight this point for the reader. I encourage you to use this service in your church or synagogue.

GOD HEARS THE CRY OF THE POOR

Leader: Lord, you are my God...The poor and the helpless have fled to you and have been safe in times of trouble. (Is 25:1, 4)

All: *But now I will come, says God, because the needy are oppressed and the persecuted groan in pain. I will give them the security they long for.* (Ps 12:5)

Leader: When that day comes...the poor and humble people will once again find the happiness which the Lord, the holy God of Israel, gives. (Is 29:18-19)

All: *The needy will not always be neglected; the hope of the poor will not be crushed forever.* (Ps 9:18)

Leader: When my people in their need look for water, when their throats are dry with thirst, then I, your God will answer their prayer; I, the God of Israel, will never abandon them. (Is 41:17)

All: *I will satisfy her poor with food.* (Ps 132:15)

Leader: Sing to God! Praise God! Who rescues the oppressed from the power of evil. (Jr 20:13)

All: *If in any of the towns in the land that God is giving you there is a brother or sister in need, then do not be selfish and refuse to help. Instead, be generous and lend as much as is needed.* (Dt 15:7-8)

Leader: When you harvest your fields, do not cut the grain at the edges of the fields, and do not go back to cut the heads of grain that were left. Do not go back through your vineyard to gather grapes that were missed or to pick up the grapes that have fallen. Leave them for poor people and foreigners. I am the Lord your God. (Lv 19:9-10)

All: *Every third year, give the tithe—a tenth of your crops—to the...stranger, the orphan, and the widow, so that in every community they will have all they need to eat.* (Dt 26:12)

Leader: Listen to this, you that trample on the needy and try to destroy the poor of the country. (Am 8:4)

All: *Let justice flow like a stream, and righteousness like a river that never goes dry.* (Am 5:24)

Leader:	The kind of fasting I want is this: remove the chains of oppression and the yoke of injustice, and let the oppressed go free. Share your food with the hungry and open your homes to the homeless poor. (Is 58:6-7)
All:	*My heart praises the Lord; my soul is glad because of God my Savior...God has filled the hungry with good things, and sent the rich away with empty hands.* (Lk 1:46-47, 53)
Leader:	The Spirit of God is upon me, because God has chosen me to bring good news to the poor. God has sent me to proclaim liberty to the captives and recovery of sight to the blind, to set free the oppressed and announce that the time has come when God will save all people. (Lk 4:18-19)
All:	*Happy are you poor; the Reign of God is yours! Happy are you who are hungry now; you will be filled! Happy are you who weep now; you will laugh.* (Lk 6:20-21)
Leader:	Watch out and guard yourselves from every kind of greed; because a person's true life is not made up of the things possessed, no matter how rich he or she may be. (Lk 12:15)
All:	*There was once a rich man who dressed in the most expensive clothes and lived in great luxury every day. There was also a poor man named Lazarus, covered with sores, who used to be brought to the rich man's door, hoping to eat bits of food that fell from the rich man's table.* (Lk 16:19-21)
Leader:	I was hungry and you fed me, thirsty and you gave me drink. (Mt 25:35)
All:	*There was no one in the group who was in need. Those who owned fields or houses would sell them, bring the money received from the sale, and turn it over to the apostles; and the money was distributed to each one according to his or her needs.* (Ac 4:34-35)

Leader: Do not forget to do good and to help one another, because these are the sacrifices that please God. (He 13:16)

All: *This is how we know what love is: Christ gave his life for us. We too, then, ought to give our lives for our brothers and sisters. If a rich person sees someone in need yet has a closed heart, how can that person claim that he or she loves God? My children, our love should not be just in words and talk; it must be true love which shows itself in action.* (Jn 3:16-18)

Leader: After this I looked, and there was an enormous crowd—no one could count all the people! They were from every race, tribe, nation, and language, and they stood in front of the throne of the Lamb... (Rev 7:9)

All: *Never again will they hunger or thirst; neither sun nor any scorching heat will burn them, because the Lamb, who is in the center of the throne, will be their shepherd, and the lamb will guide them to springs of life-giving water. And God will wipe away every tear from their eyes.* (Rev 7:16-17)

The response of religion to the cry of the poor is seen in the tradition of our churches and synagogues. At the annual Seder feast, an extra place is left at the table for the stranger, the wayfarer, the widow, the neighbor who cannot afford such a celebration.

Christian churches during the Middle Ages owned a "parish house" to provide a place of shelter for individuals and families in need of temporary housing.

Today groups like Catholic Charities, Jewish Community Services and Lutheran Community Services reach out daily to those in need. Pope John Paul II reflects this urgency in his Encyclical Letter *On Social Concern* of December 30, 1989. "...this love of preference for the poor, and the decisions which it inspires in us, cannot but embrace the immense multitudes of the hungry, the needy, the homeless, those without medical care, and above all, those without hope of a better future. It is impossible not to take account of the existence of these realities."

An Interfaith Response

At the beginning, it was primarily the Catholic churches which responded with donations and volunteers. Within the first year, Protestant churches became involved in the same way. During the last two years, Jewish congregations have joined us.

Many religious congregations collect food for us. They sometimes sponsor fundraisers and send the proceeds to us. For example, a nearby Catholic school sent in this letter:

> Dear Mike, I am delighted to enclose a check for $107 to help support your work with the homeless. Last week, one of the vendors who services St. Raphael School donated 15 cases of popcorn. We sold the popcorn to the students and told them that the proceeds would be used to help the homeless as part of our observation of Respect Life Month. Several first graders bought the popcorn and were entitled to change, but told us to keep the change for the homeless! I'm pleased that our children seem to be responding so well to the Gospel challenge to care for all of God's people. Our gift is small, but it comes to you and the people you serve with lots of love!

More than a quarter of all donations come from churches and synagogues. Occasionally a church will be especially generous. For example, when we were purchasing the Mary Brennan INN, St. Joseph's Church in Garden City gave us $16,000 towards its acquisition. When a member of the parish council attacked the pastor for his overzealous generosity with parish funds, the pastor stated: "Listen, when we are generous towards poor people, that's the most important thing we can do." At another time, the United Church in Rockville Centre gave us a no-interest loan to purchase the Rosa Parks INN.

We certainly appreciate receiving food and money, but we rejoice most when people come to lend a hand. I've been invited to speak at over 100 churches and synagogues within the past three years. I always put in a plug for volunteers. And you know something, we get them!

Sometimes the volunteers come to us individually. That's good because then they have a chance to meet volunteers from other religions and they are freer to mingle with our guests.

Many times they come as a group from their church or synagogue. For example, in the Freeport INN, different churches have taken responsibility for specific days of the week. The Social Concerns committee from St. Boniface Church in Sea Cliff prepare supper in their homes on the third Saturday of each month and serve the food at Hospitality INN that night. The Reconstructionist Temple of Roslyn sends a crew over each Sunday morning to prepare and serve brunch at one of our shelters. The youth group from St. Mary's in Manhasset comes once a month to prepare supper in Hospitality INN. Mel Greenberg from Temple Beth El, Great Neck, frequently calls and asks where we need volunteers because his Social Concerns group wants to help. Last year a coalition of two temples from West Hempstead made it possible to supply volunteers to cover our Mary Brennan INN night shelter every Tuesday evening from 7 p.m. until 7 a.m. the following morning. The Confirmation class from St. Joachim and Anne's Church in Cedarhurst held a walk-a-thon for the hungry and homeless and all proceeds were sent to The INN.

Several years ago I was invited to speak at the Garden City Jewish Center. Before I addressed the congregation, the rabbi suggested a superb way to get his people to volunteer. "Tell them it would be a marvelous work of charity and justice to offer the use of part of our temple as a shelter for the homeless!" With fear and trepidation I told the group: "I'd like to suggest that you invite The INN to use some of your space here as an emergency shelter." I heard a slight gasp in the audience. "There are two reasons why you should do this. First of all, when Long Island hears that a congregation in beautiful Garden City is accepting the homeless, we'll shame other towns into it? And secondly, remember when this temple first came to Garden City it was met by prejudice and hatred? Well, if you now open your doors to the homeless, you'll really go down in history!" They laughed, but we never received an invitation to set up shop there.

Our general experience with religious groups is that they are most generous with their money and time, but when we attempt to move them from the stance of charity to one of justice, they don't want to hear it. Especially if it's a matter of advocating affordable housing. I'm afraid we've done well in teaching our religious congregations how to be good fundraisers and donors, but not how to do *justice* for the poor. That is why we must urge our religious leaders to preach justice for the poor.

The Church must be on the cutting edge. It is our church people who must awaken the conscience of society, in particular, our elected officials. This might mean alienating some members of the congregation who believe that religion has no place in politics. It was Ghandi who said: "Those who say that religion has nothing to do with politics know neither religion nor politics." Didn't Jesus and the prophets speak often and adamantly to the political leaders of the day, chastising them for ignoring the needs of the poor? Our preachers today must take risks and urge their congregations to raise a choral cry to heaven on behalf of the poor—a cry which will shake the thrones of those in power!

On April 3, 1968, in his last public address on the eve of his assassination, Martin Luther King urged his fellow preachers to address the here-and-now needs of the poor. In the speech entitled *I See the Promised Land*, he told them: "It's alright to talk about 'long white robes over yonder,' in all of its symbolism. But ultimately people want some suits and dresses and shoes to wear down here. It's alright to talk about 'streets flowing with milk and honey,' but God has commanded us to be concerned about the slums down here, and his children who can't eat three square meals a day."

How can our diverse religious congregations put more than a dent in the problem of homelessness? If it is true (and our shelter provider advocates truly believe it is) that the chief cause of homelessness is the lack of affordable housing for low income people, here is a way that the churches and synagogues can help.

The Nassau Suffolk Coalition for the Homeless is asking dioceses, parishes, and synagogues to put money into a fund which will be used by not-for-profit agencies to build and repair permanent rental housing for poor people. We have asked religious groups for direct grants or no-interest/low-interest loans to go into a "building pot" which the Coalition would administer. This very action was taken by a group of East Brooklyn churches and it occasioned the building of the Nehemiah Project— 2,000 single-family homes which were purchased by low-income people. Bishop Mugavero, the Roman Catholic Bishop of Brooklyn contributed the first no-interest loan of three million dollars. This was matched by a one-million dollar loan from the Episcopal Diocese of Long Island. Another four million in loans were contributed by the St. Paul Community Baptist Church, various religious congregations and other sources. These religious groups put enough pressure on government and business that Mayor Koch donated city land on which to build the houses, and the corporate community came forward with grants and loans to complete the project. Today 2,000 families inhabit these houses and not one of the original families has lost its house due to a mortgage default.

The Coalition's goal is to gather enough loan money that we can build homes which can be rented to poor people. How does that work? Anyone on public assistance receives a monthly shelter (rent) grant from the Department of Social Services and combined with money from the Federal Government (Section 8 grants) will supply market-value rent for each of these houses. This rent will be used to keep the house in proper shape, pay the operating costs, and employ a case manager who will regularly visit the family to provide counseling, information and referral.

We are excited about this project. It will only happen if the churches and synagogues support it. Together we can change a social problem—we can provide respectable housing for the homeless. Religious congregations can bring about this miracle of justice-making. Our religious leaders must take the lead. Do they have any other choice in the face of today's social injustice towards the poor?

Challenging the ISMS

A final reality which The INN faces consists of challenging the *isms*—racism, sexism, ageism and classism— immoral institutions in our society.

Racism

The INN challenges strong racist attitudes on Long Island. Through our integrated network of food programs and housing opportunities, we proclaim that it is not only possible but desirable for people of different races to live, learn, eat and socialize together in harmony. Since our shelter guests are racially mixed, about half black and half white, with a sprinkling of Hispanics, they are immediately placed in a situation of forced integration. It's amazing what a little bit of openness can do! When our guests first arrive, we can see the apprehension in their eyes. Some verbalize, "But I've never sat at table with a black." In most cases, these misgivings give way to receptivity and friendliness. And you'd be amazed at the cross-cultural learning which takes place around the dinner table. We often enjoy tasting foods from different countries. Our southern blacks will treat us to southern fried chicken and collard greens, our West Indians to roti, and of course for St. Patrick's Day we welcome corned beef and cabbage!

Our shelter neighbors must be perplexed by the different shades of people who emerge from our front door. Although our shelters are always in integrated neighborhoods, ours is often the only home on the block to mix and match colors within!

Our volunteers are often amazed at our racial combinations and they surprise themselves at their own reaction. Fear of those who are different disappears as stories are shared around the dinner table. We have here a microcosm of what the macrocosm should be—an oasis of cultural sharing, learning how to blend, while respecting our differences. How wonderful if this could spread throughout the world!

Sexism (and Heterosexism)

There are certain roles which our society tells us are reserved for men and others which are strictly for women. Most of this sexism breaks down in our shelters.

The household tasks are shared by males and females alike. The man who says he's never dried a dish in his life is politely handed a dishtowel. The woman who has never said grace before meals because "that's the man's job," is introduced to a new world beyond patriarchy.

Our communities of live-in volunteers are often mixed. Decisions are made based on collegiality; no one is *boss*. Leadership roles are shared. We attempt to discover each other's gifts and to encourage their growth.

In all our prayer times together, whether at community prayer in the morning, grace before meals, or an occasional communal worship service, we are careful to use inclusive language, whether in reference to people or to God, since God is neither male or female, but rather a perfect combination of the best masculine and feminine qualities.

We strive to fight against bigotry of every kind, including attitudes which smack of heterosexism, i.e., that heterosexual is the only way to be. When a leading church layman called to complain that The INN welcomes members of Dignity (a gay and lesbian association), I politely told him that all God's people are welcome to minister with and for the homeless. We all need healing— gay and straight, homeowners and homeless alike. God brings people together and small miracles are worked in relationships. Rather than condemn each other, let's work towards an open sharing and understanding which brings about peace on earth.

Ageism

The INN actively thwarts the common belief that being young is everything and being old is a curse. We welcome volunteers of all ages, from grammar school children to octogenarians. As a matter of fact, our best volunteers are people who have experienced financial difficulty or personal crisis. They can empathize best with our guests whose shattered lives bring them to our door. Some of our most effective volunteers are in their eighties and vividly remember personal hunger and need associated with the Depression. They are kind and gentle as they recall stories of their own pain while our guests listen with rapt attention and personal identification. A real bond develops.

Just recently a retired Sister came to our soup kitchen from a convent just two blocks away. She said: "I'm tired of sitting around doing nothing. I know I can serve soup." She has encouraged another retired Sister to volunteer and she's now challenging a principal to get students involved. The principal is hesitant because she doesn't think the upper-middle class parents would appreciate their children mixing with the lower class. Our retired Sister-volunteer exclaimed, "My, you've come a long way from your immigrant parents—but I'm not sure if it's up or down!"

Classism

Which brings me to my final point: The INN directly combats classism—a materialistic attitude which says more is better. In our society, one's worth is too often based on one's bank account. There are rigid lines between rich and poor. What's frightening to those who work with the homeless is that these divisions are narrowing, while the gap between rich and poor grows wider every day. It is prominently evident in Grand Central Station as wealthy Wall Street executives walk past hordes of homeless people.

The INN attempts to bring together people of different classes to learn that underneath the quality of clothing is an equalizing quality of heart. We need to get beyond the externals associated with class division to what's on the inside: values, dreams, sensitivities, spirituality. Hearts are converted when the wife of a Garden City executive sits down with a welfare mother and her three children. The best compliment received by a volunteer from a guest is: "I thought you were one of us and now after our conversation, I *know* you're one of us." Why let money divide us when there are so many other human values to unite us?

ISMS have a unique, sinister way of dividing people.

The INN tries to bring people together by leaving these *isms* at the door.

Beyond The ISMS

How can a little INN take on city hall? The name of the game is systemic change. It is only through changing our institutions that the injustices perpetrated on the voiceless and powerless poor will be rectified. To feed and shelter the homeless is only the beginning. We must go beyond this to make the poor independent of handouts.

Our elected officials continue to give *charity* to the homeless. It's when we confront the system (government, church or the isms) that they get nervous. Then it's a difficult job that doesn't get votes, e.g., raising the minimum wage, expanding day-care services, providing health care and affordable housing for poor people. Yet, that's what our God calls us to do—secure *justice* for the most vulnerable.

Is it like David fighting Goliath? Yes it is, and again, David will win!

Epilogue

As I conclude *Give Them Shelter* allow me to return to the dedication page of this book:

> This book is dedicated to the hungry and homeless people on Long Island...they are us, and we are them.

What do I mean by this statement?

They are us. I hope that in reading this book you have discovered and now believe that there truly are homeless people on Long Island. The problem is with us and it is growing daily. We are all in it together—wealthy, middle class, and poor people on Long Island. The homeless are not imports from New York City, but long-time residents of Nassau and Suffolk Counties. Since we are neighbors, we are responsible for each other. We must reach out to our hurting sisters and brothers. But we must also extend our awareness to fellow Long Islanders who either aren't aware of the problem, or who choose not to acknowledge it. Finally, we must awaken the consciences of our elected officials and demand that they address this shameful epidemic of homelessness on affluent Long Island.

We are them. Let's start with imagining that "we could be them." For many of us are or know someone who is only two or three paychecks away from hunger and homelessness. Due to the rising cost of living we are seeing more and more of a split between the classes and more who are sliding through the cracks. This division is readily apparent as one drives south on Franklin Avenue from Garden City into Hempstead. In the course of one mile the scene changes from sumptuous wealth to abject poverty.

The working poor can easily slip through the cracks. All it takes is one financial setback, being laid off, an accident or sickness and a person can go from living in an apartment to living in his or her car. We see more and more of these people in our shelter. Indeed, *we* could easily become *them*.

Yet, in another sense...*we are them*.

There are many types of homelessness. I have experienced feelings of homelessness when I haven't felt loved, when I was lonely, when I felt left out, when I lacked self-acceptance and self-worth. Mother Teresa reflected upon this expanded sense of homelessness in the following excerpt from her book, *Words to Love By*:

> Hungry not only for bread
> — but hungry for love
> Naked not only for clothing
> — but naked of human dignity and respect
> Homeless not only for want of a room of bricks
> — but homeless because of rejection.

Every time you have these feelings of inner homelessness, pause and unite yourself in spirit with the physically homeless. Walk in their shoes for a while. We are them in more ways than we like to admit.

Hope In The Midst Of Despair

In light of the homelessness which surrounds us, both the physical homelessness we see on Long Island, as well as the poverty of spirit which causes so much pain, how do we face each new day with hope?

People often ask me: "Don't you get overwhelmed, depressed or cynical in the face of all these homeless and broken people? How do you manage to carry on with a positive attitude day after day?"

In reflecting upon my own experiences, I've identified five sources of light, or lightness, in living my life among homeless people:

The *smile* on the face of a shelter guest. I remember Susan who said as she left one of our shelters after a stay of four weeks: "Thanks for my time here. Besides feeding and sheltering me, you surrounded me with the support and love I used to get from my family. I want my home to be just like this one—filled with laughter and acceptance for all." If we could help just one guest each day in this profound way, we would have succeeded. The smiles encourage us and bless us with life.

The *hands* of others. I am continually inspired by the deeds and lives of all those who help at the INN—from the staff, to live-in community members, to the multitude of volunteers. Where else could I be surrounded with such loving people? I keep meeting people in the business world whose jobs and lives are a heavy burden. I come home to the shelter to find the kind of people who are enlivened in their work with the homeless. So many of those who have come to give, find that they receive much more.

Homeless people have a way of inspiring, enlightening, educating and converting us. That's their ministry and we are the happy beneficiaries.

The power of our work is strengthened by *prayer*. I fully believe that our outreach to the homeless is of God. Interfaith prayer is crucial to what we do. As The INN grew and I was spending sleepless nights wondering how we could manage the growing giant, I turned to God and said, "OK, I'm doing all I can. But I can't oversee all the details. It's too much. You must help." As soon as I said that I relaxed in the knowledge that God is with us.

Besides individual prayer, from time to time we sponsor a retreat for our volunteers. A day of reflection away from our soup kitchens and shelters does a world of good for clearing the head, pooling the strengths of many, and taking the time to remember that from our diverse backgrounds God has joined us in this noble interfaith ministry.

Since the inception of The INN, I have had a recurring and persistent wish. Whenever I'd see an overworked staff person, a tired live-in shelter community member or an overburdened volunteer, I would think: "Imagine if someday The INN could have a special place away from all this madness, a place for quiet reflection and renewal."

That dream is about to become a reality. Thanks to the generosity of donors, The INN will soon be the proud owner of a house in Weston, Vermont. Set in the natural beauty of the Green Mountain National Forest, two miles from a priory of hospitable Benedictine Monks with a daily prayer schedule open to the public, there is a sprawling house which will become The INN Reflection Center. Groups of staff and shelter community members, as well as volunteers and some homeless guests, will come to this country spot for interfaith, interracial, and inter-class prayer and sharing. This sacred spot will be a place of peace—sometimes silent, sometimes filled with shared laughter.

Isn't this, after all, what separates The INN from other social service agencies? We have always celebrated interfaith prayer and relationships as our cornerstones. Our trust in God is what continues to give us hope, even in the face of the growing epidemic of homelessness on affluent Long Island. We know that God, who has a special concern for fringe people and those rejected by society, will protect these favorite ones.

Living at the shelter with a *community* of volunteers enriches my life and strengthens me daily. I'm especially fortified as we pray together each morning. I am amazed at our variety of prayer styles. It's a special time of togetherness and a reminder that we do what we do only with God's help. Tuesday evenings are sacred too, for on that night at Hospitality INN the community sets all other business aside, and we enjoy each other's company. It's what we call "at home night" and that's when our real need for family is satisfied.

We're in it together and through our prayer we hope to make it work. I'm bolstered by the joy and love of this special community of people in my life.

Finding the *humor* in a situation makes all the difference. Life at The INN is not all gloomy. We'd sink under the weight of it all if we concentrated on the depressing aspects of homelessness and never looked at the bright side. We laugh a lot—at ironic situations, at the innocent remarks of children and at ourselves! I have a natural funny streak; if I can't laugh, I can't survive.

Take for example, the time a live-in community member was leading morning prayer. Chris is a medical student. He meant to say "We will now have meditation." But influenced by his trade he prayed, "We will now have medication." We laughed through the rest of morning prayer!

To Sum Up

The ministry of The INN can be summed up in the following points of our official Mission Statement:

The Interfaith Nutrition Network (INN) is a not-for-profit, volunteer-based organization on Long Island. It was organized to address the problems of hunger and homelessness with empathy and understanding by:

— Feeding the hungry in safe, clean, caring environments with no questions asked.

— Providing emergency and transitional shelter for the homeless in dignified, home-like atmospheres.

— Exploring the ways and means to establish long-term shelters and permanent, low-cost housing.

— Educating the public and the political structure as to the extent of hunger and homelessness and the needs of those who find themselves in this condition.

— Evaluating other basic needs: helping guide families and individuals to providers of medical, social, educational, career, and other services.

I hope that as you have been reading this book you have seen the natural progression of The INN. We began with one small soup kitchen which led to the opening of many more. We kept meeting people at the soup kitchen who had no home, and that brought us to the opening of one shelter, followed by many others. When we attempted to assist our guests to find permanent housing, we were shocked at the lack of decent, affordable housing for poor people and that took us in the direction of establishing, administering and maintaining permanent housing for the homeless and the working poor.

This journey has enabled us to change people's attitudes and values through education, move volunteers' hearts by meeting the homeless face-to-face and together transform the system. The latter has been accomplished because the people of The INN have convinced their elected officials to examine a system which has too often divided people with money from those who have none. The people at the bottom lack housing, health care, day care, and adequate wages to allow them to live decently and with self-respect.

Indifference to the needs of poor people is widespread throughout the social system. The INN has been moved to continually challenge the very institutions upon which our society rests: the church/synagogue, government, and the *isms:* racism, classism, sexism and ageism. The following graph gives a visual summary of the movement.

THE INN

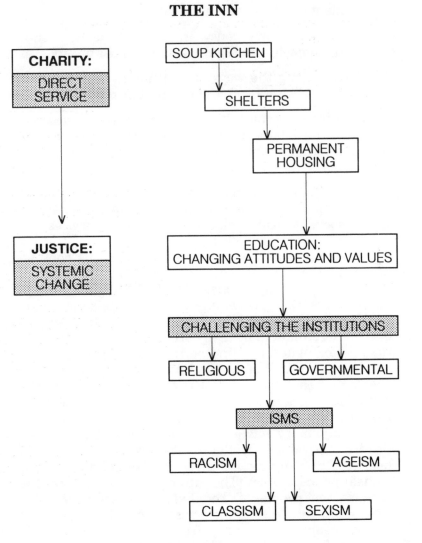

It's simple yet very complex at the same time. What began with making a pot of soup to satisfy hunger has developed into re-forming people's attitudes and to the potential healing of society.

This tremendous opportunity and challenge to empower God's favorites, the poor, can only bring us to our knees in prayer:

A LAMENTATION

GOD, you have led us from serving soup to systemic
           change.
How could you have done this to us?
We simply wanted to serve others, not change ourselves.
You are a demanding God, moving us not-so-gently from
           charity to justice.
Yet, if nothing is too good for your favorites, the anawim
I must be like them too—to know what it is to be rejected.
Save me from drowning in my own good intentions.
Sometimes I feel so homeless!
Let me find a home, O God, in you.

Finally, true prayer leads naturally to action. We must be ready to take strong stands on behalf of the needs and rights of the homeless.

Let us be inspired by the words of Mother Jones, a great advocate for poor people in Appalachia. This spirit-filled woman once said: "Let's pray for the dead, and fight like hell for the living."

Other Resurrection Press Publications

Of Life and Love. Fr. Jim Lisante. Foreword by John Powell. Preface by Archbishop Roger Mahony. $4.95

Award-winning columnist Fr. Jim Lisante offers his words of wisdom and encouragement in his first full-length book. Whatever your age, wherever you are in life, Fr. Jim's timely writings on Family Matters and Respect Life issues will challenge and inspire you.

"Excellent spiritual reading for parents, teens and teachers." *Praying*

RVC Liturgical Series

Brief, easy-to-read books for those actively involved in liturgical ministry or who simply wish better to understand the Catholic liturgy.

Now available:

Our Liturgy: Your Guide to the Basics. Describes and discusses the varieties of Liturgical Ministry and clearly explains Liturgical Objectives and Order of Mass.
$4.25

The Great Seasons: Your Guide to Celebrating.
Offers valuable insights to help with parish liturgy planning and to deepen private celebration of Advent, the Christmas Season, Lent, the Triduum and Easter Season.
$3.25

Coming soon:

The Liturgy of the Hours: Your Guide to Praying.
An informative introduction to praying the Divine Office, with practical suggestions for parish implementation.

The Lector's Ministry: Your Guide to Proclaiming the Word. Not only gives practical advice but also discusses the Scripture-rooted spirituality required of a lector.

Our Spirit-Life Collection
of Audio Cassettes

Our *Spirit Life Collection* of audiocassettes brings you the most up-to-date information on religious, ethical and moral issues. Listening at home or in the car—alone or in a group—will uplift, educate and challenge you to walk the walk of committed discipleship.

Praying on Your Feet: A Contemporary Spirituality for Active Christians. Fr. Robert Lauder. 45 min. $5.95

Have you ever felt guilty about being too busy to pray? Fr. Lauder assures us that spirituality in today's world can be achieved on our feet as well as on our knees.

Annulment: Healing-Hope-New Life.
Msgr. Thomas Molloy.
60 min. $5.95

In lay language Msgr. Molloy unravels the myth and mystery surrounding the annulment process. "A healing process, a time for meaningful reflection, growth and new beginnings."

Divided Loyalties: Church Renewal through a Reformed Priesthood.
Anthony T. Padovano, Ph.D. S.T.D.
60 min. $6.95

In this thought-provoking and timely reflection on today's Church, Dr. Padovano exhorts us to fashion a new Church. His keen historical perspectives, powerful analogies and loving example of service will inspire you to make the Church a credible Church where hope, truth and mercy prevail.

ALL ROYALTIES FROM THE SALE OF THIS BOOK GO TO THE SUPPORT OF THE INN

If your organization desires to use this book as a fund-raiser for The INN contact:

Resurrection Press Ltd.
P.O. Box 248
Williston Park, NY 11596
(516) 742-5686

Discounts are available on bulk orders.

For more information about The INN

..... To volunteer

..... To arrange for a speaker

..... To make a contribution

THE INN
148 Front Street
Hempstead, NY 11550
(516) 486-8506